Walking in Grandpa's Footsteps
Stories of God's Grace and Mercy

Robert Loran Ford

All Rights Reserved © Robert Loran Ford, 2019

His Way Publishing

Winston-Salem, NC

Dedication

This book is dedicated to the one person who taught me more about parenting than I wanted to know – my daughter, Lauran Gayle Ford Mosser. I was with her mother in the labor & delivery room throughout the early morning hours of November 17, 1981. Finally, at 9:20 am she decided to come out into the world. From that point on, life would never be the same again. She challenged us to be longsuffering and forgiving, along with a number of other skills not listed here.

Neither her mother nor I have any regrets. She brought a special bond and dimension to our family. We loved her from the moment we set eyes on her, since she is our one and only. Spoiled! Yes, some, I guess!

Our daughter has a family of her own and has been an excellent mother and homemaker in addition to starting her own business. She has made us proud in so many ways.

Today her daughter, Taylor Loran Mosser, is teaching Lauran and Jason the art of parenting. From my observations, I believe that they are fast learners. Keep up the good work!

Acknowledgments

The response I have received from the publication of my first book, *Behind Grandma's Apron Strings: Stories of God's Grace and Mercy*, was beyond my expectations. I did not expect the book to make the impact it did on the life of those who found a common ground within the stories. It has been this response that has inspired me to write this book.

My longtime friend, The Reverend Dennis Hester, has in no way played a small part in this endeavor. Even with his busy schedule, he has taken the time to guide me through this process. His publishing company, *His Way Publishing*, has provided excellent service.

Through this process, I have enlisted the services of various people to proofread the manuscript. Dr. Rick Vandett, former superintendent of Hickory City Schools, has provided valuable feedback on my use of the English language.

To my family and friends who have been the inspiration of many of the devotions, I can't thank you enough for sharing your lives with me. God has worked through you in unique ways. You have been a blessing to me.

My wife, Gail, who has always supported me and who has given me many suggestions concerning the devotions, has provided invaluable service for this publication. She has been an inspiration for me to do what God has called me to do.

Foreword

Throughout our lives, each of us can remember incidents from our childhood that impacted our adult lives. Some of us have said at one time or another, "I wish I had written down some of the things that happened in my life, because I could have learned some valuable lessons." Since most of us never take the time to record those events, they often fade into the recesses of our minds. On the other hand, Robert Loran Ford has taken the time to reach into his memories and recall the many events of his past that have impacted his life. He has found the hidden presence of God at work.

Robert has a dry sense of humor and a self-deprecating nature that come out in his retelling of how God's mercy and grace were evident throughout his life. As you read each vignette, you will find yourself reflecting on how God's grace and mercy have been evident in similar events on your journey through life. You, too, may come to realize how God has revealed Himself in the mundane events of your life.

I have had the pleasure of working alongside Robert as we try to help homeless and needy veterans in our community. At our weekly meeting, Robert ends each session with a short homily about how God works in our lives. All of us leave those meetings in a positive, hopeful frame of mind, thanks to Robert's insights on discovering God in unfamiliar places.

Read this book for the discoveries you may make, for the insights you may receive and just for the pure enjoyment of the God moments.

Ric Vandett

Retired School Superintendent

Colleague of Robert

4 ROBERT FORD

The Foothills Veterans Helping Veterans

Hickory, NC

WALKING IN GRANDPA'S FOOTSTEPS: STORIES OF GOD'S GRACE AND MERCY

Table of Contents

1. Walking in Grandpa's Footsteps

2. A Bad Influence

3. A Big Black Cauldron

4. A Flying Coke Bottle

5. A Friend at My Window

6. A Hidden Village

7. A Horse and Carriage

8. A Kite Gone Bad

9. A Man Running After Me

10. A Pointing Finger

11. A Tough Shot to Handle

12. Abandoned

13. Basic Training

14. Broken Bones

15. Bucket List

16. Caught in the Act

17. Do You Have a Light

18. Do You Want to Dance

19. Fighting with Bruce Cooper

20. Giving Your Life Away

21. God is Out to Get Me

22. Humpty the Egg

23. I Was Lost

24. Deep Sea Fishing

25. Mistaken Identity

26. My Brother's Keeper

27. Rough and Tumble

28. Santa Lied

29. Searching for Snakes

30. She Had a Dream

31. She's Still My Friend

32. Stranded

33. Summer Games

34. Swim or Drown

35. Telling It Like It Is

36. The Big Explosion

37. The Breezeway

38. The Bunkmate from Hell

39. The Chase

40. The Drive-In Theater

41. The House on the Hill

42. The Mysterious Casket

43. The Times! They Are a Changing

44. The Way It Was

45. Tipping Over Canoes

46. Two Red Shirts

47. Which Way Should I Go?

48. Why God Made Dogs

49. Your Arms Are Too Short

50. The Request

Introduction

The ways that God is at work in our lives are like sand on a beach, too many to count. Each of us has stories to tell about our journey through life. It is the most prominent events that stand out in our minds. Looking deeper into these events, we can begin to uncover this mysterious presence of God. Like Jacob's discovery, "God was in his life, and he knew it not."

The devotions are filled with these events and examples of how God is at work making Himself known to us. For the most part, the stories are real and tell of actual events happening to people in everyday life situations. The one devotion, "Humpty the Egg," is a fantasy with some powerful implications.

There are numerous ways in which all of us are connected. The fact that we all have experienced some breakage in our life is a most powerful connection. The devotions seek to expose this common ground and to ensure us that we are not the last of the Mohicans. Nor are we the only one in our canoe, as it makes its way down the life's river with its zigzags and turns. If we look around, we will find others in the canoe making the trip with us.

I believe that God is always where He needs to be. Therefore, God calls us to come and participate in what He is already doing to bring healing and wholeness to life. I pray that the devotions will help you to hear His summons upon your life, and that you will discover the possibilities that are before you.

Enjoy the book!

Robert Loran Ford

WALKING IN GRANDPA'S FOOTSTEPS: STORIES OF GOD'S GRACE AND MERCY

1

Walking in Grandpa's Footsteps

It was back in the days when this southern town in western North Carolina got snow every year. This year was no exception. The town had received about seven or eight inches of the white stuff. One day when my parents and I were visiting with my grandparents, we were sitting in the living room with the big potbellied stove going full blast, but the coal bucket was running low. When it came to heating a home, coal was king. Seeing that the coal bucket was about empty, Grandpa was getting ready to go outside to the coal pile. Not wanting to miss a good opportunity to be out in the snow, I announced that I wanted to go, too. Grandpa was reluctant at first, but my persistence paid off and I was allowed to take the trip with him.

On the front porch, Grandpa instructed me to follow in his footsteps. As an eight-year-old, I thought that was doable. So, off we went! Although Grandpa was not a big man by any stretch of the imagination, he took very small steps in order to make it easier for me to follow. The trip to the coal pile and back was uneventful, except for Grandpa's repeated requests for me to get out of the snow and come into the house, which I eventually did! There would be other days we would be together, which I look back on with fond memories.

Grandpa Ford—M.A. Ford, as he was known in the community—was a good conversationalist. He listened as well as he talked. He was a touchy-feely sort of person. His voice was soft and gentle to the ears, and I don't ever remember seeing him angry. Overall, he set a good example for us grandkids.

When Grandpa Ford went to get his driver's license for the first time, they asked him what his middle name was. Grandpa informed them that he didn't have a middle name. So, they asked him what middle initial he would like to have. Grandpa chose the first letter of the alphabet "A." So, from then on, he was known as "M. A. Ford." The letter "M" stood for Manley.

Grandpa's most prominent characteristic was his sense of humor. He loved to laugh and to make others laugh. His repertoire of practical jokes was limitless. From time to time, when Grandpa went to town, that is the big town of Rutherfordton, he came by my parents' home for a short visit. On a number of those occasions, he let me go with him.

Lucky for me, my grandpa passed on to me his sense of humor. It has been therapeutic for me to laugh at myself and with the world around me. Laughter, I've been told by a number of doctors, triggers our body's production of dopamine, which is a feel-good chemical. The by-product of that is we feel good about ourselves, which lifts our spirits.

Yes, walking in my grandpa's footsteps has taught me a lot about life and about myself. I have regrets I didn't walk in his footsteps more often. I didn't talk to my grandparents enough about their journey through life. There were lessons to be learned and wisdom to be received. Sure, they were from another day and time, but that's what makes their life so interesting. It's like footsteps in the snow.

In the New Testament, Jesus invited some fishermen to walk in his footsteps. The Gospel according to Mark tells us the fishermen immediately dropped their nets and followed him to the cross. From that point on, they would need to take up their cross and follow God's calling for their life.

Whose footsteps are you walking in?

2

A Bad Influence

It was a Friday night and there was not a lot happening on Farley Avenue Extension near Spartanburg, South Carolina, so I decided to go up to the local café/convenience store to get a hotdog. The store didn't look like much from the outside, but the cooks there made some of the best hotdogs in town. It so happened a few of my friends were there, and at some point we got on the subject of wine. Ed Wilson, the Fonze of our group, suggested we walk up to another café located about a half-mile away, which sold a variety of alcoholic beverages.

On the way there, somehow I stuck my foot in my mouth by saying wine did not have much punch to it. Of course, that observation was coming from the mouth of a 14-year-old who did not know what wine tasted like. Ed, who was probably in his early twenties, said he would buy all the wine I would drink. It sounded like a good offer to me, so I took him up on it.

The wine of the day was called "Seven Star." It was probably the cheapest wine on the face of God's green earth. I don't know how much I drank, but on the way back home it began to hit. My ability to walk and talk was deeply impaired, but somehow the guys got me back to my house. They sat me down in a rocking chair located in our front room and turned on the TV set. It would have helped if they had pointed me in the right direction, but at that point, I don't guess it mattered.

My dad worked the third shift at Saxon Mill. Not long after being placed in my living room, I heard him getting up to get ready for work. I decided just to stay put and play it cool. Eventually, my father came into the room and took one look at me and said, "Son, you better go to bed!"

My response was something like, "OK, Dad, I think you're right!" As I tried to make my way from the living room to my bedroom, I had to pass through two other rooms.

I thought if I could make it through the door that led into the kitchen, I would have it made. I made the transition okay, but noticed a TV tray lay in my way. It was the kind of tray that was on a stand and stood about three feet off the floor. Thinking I had performed the right maneuver, I caught one of the legs of the tray with my foot and over I went. Oops, there goes another TV tray! I finally made it to my bedroom, got into bed, forgot about taking my clothes off, and turned out the light. Ah, safe and sound!

I had forgotten I was supposed to pick my mother up from work. In South Carolina at the time, you could get your driver's license at age 14. I was 14 ½! Mom worked at Spartanburg General Hospital as an LPN. I took her to work with plans to use the car to go to a movie or something. The pickup time was 11:00 PM, and it was well past that time. When I didn't show up, my mom caught a ride with a friend. Dad was going out the door when she arrived. He said something to her like, "I think your son is drunk. I sent him to bed, so you might want to check on him." I lay quietly in bed, thinking nothing would be said.

That ignorance was soon put aside when all of a sudden my bedroom light came on and Mom began to yell at me. "What have you done?" she said and at the same time pulled back my covers. Then, she reached down and grabbed me by my shoulders and began to shake me like a container of salt.

I'm telling you, this sort of treatment will always get your attention. To the best of my knowledge, I told her what had happened that night. I promised not to do it again, and said I was sorry I had disappointed her. There's a certain bond between a mother and her son, especially if the son is an only child. So, her temper was short-lived, which was to my advantage.

I'd like to say that was the last time I ever got drunk, but it was not. It happened on many occasions while I was in the Air Force. At the Airman's Club, you could get any mixed drink for 20 cents, and I think beer cost 10 cents. When I was stationed at McConnell Air Force Base in Wichita, Kansas, the Air Force provided pizzas and beer every Friday. I suppose if I was going to become an alcoholic, it would have happened during that period of time.

After returning home following my tour of duty, I continued my Air Force lifestyle for a while, but eventually I made my way back to Grace Baptist Church. It was there I began to receive some spiritual healing. The minister at my church gave me a book called *The Confessions of Saint Augustine*. Augustine lived in a wild and crazy way for a portion of his adult life. He admitted if it had not been for the prayers of his mother, he would never have made it back from his trip to the far country.

Augustine also stated the most difficult thing he ever did in his life was discover who he was. To know self is to know God! To know God is to know our destiny! Augustine went on to become one of the most influential Christian writers of all time. In spite of his misdirected life, God put him back on track and did some marvelous things through him.

Like Augustine, I began to discover God's plan for my life. Through the years, God has not given up on me. Indeed, God's bountiful grace overcame my misdirected life and accomplished some marvelous things with me.

What marvelous things does God have in mind for your life?

3

A Big Black Cauldron

Every Monday, without fail, pieces of wood were placed under a big black cauldron (a large pot). Then, the cauldron was filled with water drawn from a well located about 50 feet from the house. Soon, when the water became just the right temperature, detergent was added and then some of the dirty clothes were put in. Then, something called a "washboard" was used to get out difficult stains and dirt from the clothes. That was a process that took all day to complete and required the help of all the members of the family.

Once the clothes were cleaned, each item was put on a clothesline, which was a piece of wire stretched between two poles about 20 feet apart. The fresh air and sunshine dried the clothes. When the clothes were dry, some items needed to be ironed. Inside the house there was a fireplace that was used to cook food, provide heat on a cold day and heat an iron. The clothes to be ironed were placed on the dining-room table. Then, every 15 or 20 minutes, the iron was placed near the fireplace to reheat.

The question may be asked, "Is this what they call the 'good old days'?"

The answer to that question would be, "Yes, it was and for many reasons." The common task of washing clothes brought the family together and created a bond that lives on today. Of course, that is only one of many factors that created this special bond among the Skipper family in Polk County, North Carolina, but it does stand out as a central drawing point.

Like the clothes to be washed on wash day, our lives accumulate some dirt and grime that need to be dealt with. We all make mistakes! No one is perfect! The New Testament phrase for that is "missing the mark." We have all missed the mark in a number of ways. So, how do we get cleaned up? It is from the Prophet Isaiah that we have these words:

"Come now, and let us reason together,"

Says the Lord,

"Though your sins are like scarlet,

They shall be as white as snow;

Though they are red like crimson,

They shall be as wool."

Is. 1: 18 (KJV)

Dirty clothes, like dirty lives, prevent us from living our lives to the fullest. The dirt has a way of isolating us from ourselves, our family, and our community. The way we see ourselves makes all the difference as to how we relate to the world around us. We need to feel accepted and that our life has value and purpose. When dirt (sin) enters our lives, it has a way of isolating us from our true selves. It brings on a "spiritual amnesia."

After Adam and Eve disobeyed God, they hid in some bushes nearby in the hope that no one would find them. Then, they heard the footsteps of God, who was out looking for them. Upon finding them, God offered them clean clothes to wear. They were forgiven! They were accepted!

The Good News is we have a choice. Like others who have wrestled with what to do with their mistakes in life, each one of us has a need to do the same. We may choose to hide from them or claim them, the choice is ours. God offers all of us clean clothes to wear that will not stain and will never need ironing.

Are you in need of some clean clothes?

4

A Flying Coke Bottle

It had all started a few days before when Calvin Reese and I were going through the local trash pile on Grace Cotton Mill Village. We both spotted a baby carriage that had been discarded. Calvin got to it first and laid claim to it. But as he looked it over, he decided he didn't want it, so I took it. I noticed all the wheels were in good condition, so I was thinking of putting them on a wagon. When I let Calvin in on my plans, he began to reconsider not wanting the carriage. He wanted it back. But I said to him, "I thought you didn't want it when you threw it back on the trash pile, so it's mine now." By that time, we were at the driveway to my house, so I pushed the carriage into my yard. Knowing possession was nine-tenths of the law, I felt rather confident in my legal stance.

A few days later, I was down at Johnson's Convenience Store, perhaps buying a five-cent drink or candy bar. I had just stepped outside the store and started walking back up the road to my house when I heard someone call my name. As I turned to see who it was, a Coke bottle came crashing into my forehead just above my left eye. Blood went everywhere, and I started crying from the shock and pain of being hit so hard.

Mr. and Mrs. Johnson came running out of the store to see what had happened. The Coke bottle had actually broken and pieces were still embedded in my face and forehead. Someone went to tell my parents what had happened, so I was taken to the emergency room at Rutherford Hospital. I had a large pump knot on my forehead and a big bruise around my eye.

A lady across the street had seen Calvin throw the bottle at me, and she told my parents. I can't remember if Calvin's parents had to pay for my medical bills or not, but eventually my pump knot went away as did the bruise around my eye. I was very fortunate the bottle did not hit me directly in the eye. Apparently, Calvin was still upset about not getting the carriage back, and as he thought more about what had happened, he decided to give some payback. Here was a person I considered my friend. I did not think for a moment he would actually do something like that to me. Thus, his actions had come as a total surprise.

At some point in time, Calvin apologized for hitting me with the Coke bottle and I accepted his request for reconciliation. Calvin and I put our differences behind us and went on with our lives. We still played baseball in the cow pasture during the summer and football during the fall, but in reality, we were never very close friends again.

I believe the words of Jesus have some relevance here with regard to how we ought to "pray for our enemies and pray for those that persecute (abuse) us." Praying for our enemies is a most difficult thing to do, especially if the abuse is on-going. The teaching of Jesus becomes even more difficult when he adds we should pray for those who "Do all manner of things against us." That statement covers a multitude of actions and behaviors that cause us pain and suffering.

From the cross, we have the words of Jesus, "Father forgive them, for they know not what they do." After being beaten, spat on, cursed at, and lied about, He prayed for the forgiveness of those who hurt him. In light of what He did on the cross, and the suffering and pain He endured, how can I, in good faith, not pray and forgive those who don't like me and do all matter of things against me?

Ralph Waldo Emerson wrote:

> "Sow a thought, reap a deed!
>
> Sow a deed, reap a habit!

Sow a habit, reap a way of life!

Sow a way of life, reap a destiny!"

What seeds are you sowing?

5

A Friend at My Window

We were waiting on the front porch for the doctor to call. I had been at the doctor's office earlier that day and had some blood tests to determine if I had rheumatic fever for the third time in my life. Just out of high school, I had other plans for the summer, but it appeared those plans would not be realized. Having gone through two other times with this disease, I knew what it would mean if I, indeed, had come down with another case of rheumatic fever. It would be another summer in bed.

Eventually, the phone rang and I felt a bit of tension in my gut. Mom took the call and after a few minutes of conversation, she came to the door to inform me my worst fears had been realized. My rheumatic fever was back. So, without protest, I went into the house, put my pajamas on and got into bed.

No TV in my room. Only a radio picked up WORD-AM, the local radio station in Spartanburg, South Carolina. In addition to the radio, my room had two windows. One looked out on the space between our house and our neighbor's house—the Greenways. The other window faced Farley Avenue Extension, the main road that ran in front of my house.

Being an only child, I had to be creative in my endeavor to pass the time. I drew pictures from magazines and the newspaper. I read a lot of "funny books" when I wasn't looking out my windows. I didn't have many board games at the time, because I had given them all away to my cousins. Although I didn't have a lot of stuff to occupy my time, I had one thing that was very special to me—a friend who showed up each day.

Although I could not have visitors in the house, David came to my window every morning and throughout the day wanting to know if I needed anything from Holyfield's Convenience Store up the street. He brought me candy, drinks, and ice cream as needed. In addition to these items, he kept me informed as to what was going on in our neighborhood, along with the latest gossip. I can't say enough about what his trips to my window meant to me that summer.

Dr. Gail O'Day, dean of Wake Forest University Seminary, in her studies of the Gospel according to John, said Jesus identified three components of true friendship. First of all, it is sacrificial. Jesus stated the very best way to love another person is to be willing to put your life on the line for them. In true friendship both parties are willing to make sacrifices for the other person. Second, in true friendship, sharing is a common component. Jesus told His disciples everything the Father had given to Him, He made available to them. Third, truthfulness is a component of true friendship. Jesus said to His disciples, "Truly, truly I say to you." Being honest and true to our word is the glue that holds friends together.

That summer in bed, I discovered what kind of friend I had in David Ross. He was all I would want in a friend and more. I am convinced if God allows us to have one good friend, then we have been truly blessed. If blessed in that way, may we then be the kind of friend we ought to be to others.

Our world is in desperate need of random acts of kindness. Can it count on you?

6

A Hidden Village

In this little corner of the world located in western North Carolina, on a small cotton mill village, there lived a little boy who loved to play in the woods. One day, he discovered on the other side of these woods a small village. He had not seen this village before, because his mother would not allow him to play in the deep dark part of the woods. But, on this day, he decided to go into the woods to see what it was all about. That's when he saw the hidden village.

There was something about that kid that made him want to go and find out what this village was all about. As he made his way through the village, he soon discovered those people did not look like he did. Their skin was darker. Their hair was black. Yet, in spite of these differences, they were very friendly to him, even calling him by name. He wondered how they knew his name.

At one of the smaller buildings in this village, the door was open and he could see several ladies inside working with several machines. They were doing something with pieces of cloth. The machines made a noise that he had not heard before, but not loud enough to cause him to run away. He decided to go inside. As he stood in the doorway, one of the ladies looked up and called him by name. How did she know his name? He didn't have a clue, but the lady was friendly and invited him to come in and have a seat. So he did!

After a brief conversation, he asked about the machine she was working with. "It's a sewing machine," she replied. There was a big pedal underneath that the lady worked with her feet in a back and forth motion. That pedal allowed the needle on top to go up and down, which pushed the thread through the garment. Hanging on the wall were various shirts, pants, and dresses that had been made by these ladies.

The little boy informed the ladies he did not need a dress today, so he would move on. As he made his way through the village, he met several other people who knew his name. He kept wondering how all these folks knew him. He would ask his mother when he got back home, he decided. At one of the other homes, there was a man and a woman sitting on their front porch. They were sitting in rocking chairs, the young boy's favorite kind of chair. As he approached them, he said, "Good morning!" "Good morning to you, young man. How are you today, Bob?" Again, how did these folks know his name? So he asked them.

It seems when he was just a little baby, his mother often rocked him to sleep on the front porch. It was the custom of the folks from this village to use the road and pathway that was right in front of the little boy's house. They often stopped and talked with his mother. On just about every occasion, the boy held out his arms for them to hold him. His mother told them his name. Everyone in their village knew his name.

As he talked with this couple on their front porch, they invited him to have lunch with them. It sounded like a good idea, so the little boy took them up on their offer. In fact, most of the folks that lived in the village ate lunch at that home. At the dinner table, he was seated between Uncle Marek and Aunt Dosey, as he came to know them. Uncle Marek said the blessing over the meal and thanked God for sending the boy their way. Boy, that was the first time he had heard someone thank God for having him around. Generally, his uncles and aunts wanted him to go away.

Uncle Marek sat in what was known as a wheelchair. He had been sick as a child and could not walk. The wheelchair allowed him to get around the village to visit his family and friends. He seemed like a good man and did not seem to have any bitterness about his condition. He treated the boy like one of the family, which was amazing.

The little boy noticed a swing set at one of the homes in the village. He asked about the kids who played on the swings. Twin girls lived at that house. Their mother and father ran a restaurant that had some of the best home cooking in the country. So, with all this information, the little boy put this home on his list of places to visit. "And visit he did, on a pretty regular basis."

One day he saw the girls playing on their swing set, so he went over to make friends with them. They invited him to swing, and each of the girls took turns at giving him a push in the swing. Man that was great! The girls were older than he was, but that didn't matter to him. On occasion, the little boy and his parents went out to their family's restaurant, which was called "Jamie's." That was some of the best food he had eaten.

There are fond memories of this small village that still linger with this little boy, who is now grown up. Sitting around the table having lunch with Uncle Marick and Aunt Dosey and ther family members and feeling accepted as part of the family was a great feeling for a kid who was an only child. They liked the little boy, and he liked them.

In many ways, that is a picture of how God likes to see His people, enjoying the presence of one another around the table of fellowship. In the Book of Isaiah, the prophet wrote: "Hello out there, everyone that is thirsty, come to the waters; and you that have no money, come, buy, and eat; yes, come, buy wine and milk without money and without price." Isaiah 51:1 (Paraphrase by RLF)

If Jamie had put a sign with this on it out in front of her restaurant, how long do you think she would have been in business? Not long! Her restaurant would have needed unlimited resources to pull that off. That is the point Isaiah attempted to make. God's resources are unlimited. Israel (the Northern Kingdom) had been defeated in war. The land lay waste. How could His people ever get back on their feet? The Lord would provide. The Annual Feast of Tabernacles, celebrated at the end of the harvest season to commemorate the days their forefathers spent in the wilderness, stood as a reminder their God was still in the business of taking care of them.

In the Gospel according to Luke, Jesus told a story about a certain man who prepared a great banquet and invited all his friends: "A certain man made a great supper, and invited his friends to attend. He sent out his servants at suppertime to remind them it was time for supper. But they all began to make excuses saying why they couldn't attend. One said, "I have bought a piece of land, and I must go and see about it."

Another said, "I have bought five yoke of oxen, and I must go to check on them."

Still another said, "I just got married, therefore, I can't come tonight."

So, the servants went back and told their master about the excuses. Then the master of the house, being somewhat upset with this news, sent his servants out again with orders to go into the streets and lanes of the city to bring the poor, and the maimed, and the blind to the supper! The servants informed their master there was still more room in the banquet hall. Again, the master of the house issued an order: "Go out into the highways and byways and compel them to come in that my house may be filled!" Luke 14: 16b – 23 (Paraphrase by RLF)

There is always room for one more around God's supper table. The food never runs out, and as at the wedding at Cana, (John 2: 1) the wine barrels are always full. No one is left out! All are invited. Do you have time for communion with God today?

7

A Horse and Carriage

It was the community event of the summer! Cooper's Gap Baptist Church located in Polk County, North Carolina, was hosting a gospel singing. Gospel groups from around the area would have an opportunity to perform. The majority of the community would be there, whether they liked gospel music or not, for it was a time to socialize with folks you did not often see.

Gardner Skipper had his eye on one of the local girls and was planning to ask her to go with him to the singing. Gardner went by the home of Bernice Wilson to get permission from her father, Loran Wilson, to take her to the singing, and apparently the answer he got was "Yes." With help from Gardner, Bernice climbed up into the buggy and off they went. I can imagine the dust coming up from the dirt road as the horse and buggy made its way down the pathway.

On the way back from Cooper's Gap later that Sunday afternoon, as the horse slowly made its way up one hill and down another, Gardner decided to make his move on Bernice. He slowly placed his arm on the back of the carriage seat, mindful not to touch her but just to position his arm in a strategic location. For a moment he thought his plan had worked, but he soon discovered his actions had not gone unnoticed by Bernice.

Bernice turned to Gardner and said, "Stop the buggy right now, and I'll get out and walk the rest of the way home." Gardner quickly removed his arm from the back of the seat and apologized for his mistake. I suppose the apology was accepted, since they continued to see one another and eventually got married. A relationship that started out on shaky ground eventually got back on the right track. Together, they raised eight children.

Imagine! On the first date, my grandfather was not allowed to put his arm around my grandmother. Many folks today would say they were moving way too slowly in their relationship. My grandparents would say the world today is moving much too fast. The question, "Can I put my arm around my sweetheart?" has been replaced today with "Can we move in together?"

In the song recorded by Percy Sledge, "Take Time to Know Her," his mother gave him some good advice about his relationship with his girlfriend, but he ignored it. The end result was that he kept on getting hurt by girlfriends who were not faithful to him. The old saying stands true: if we do not learn from our mistakes then we are destined to repeat them over and over again. What Percy sings leaves us with some good advice: "Take time to know the person we think we might like to hitch our wagon to."

The Bee Gees, in their song, "How Deep Is Your Love," seek to determine if the love they are experiencing from another person is just a surface love or has a deeper component to it. Perhaps this, too, is an important issue to determine, if we plan to live the rest of our lives with another person.

If a lifetime commitment is made, then it should in some way take on the character as described in the song, "Love and Marriage" recorded by Frank Santira and written by James Van Heusen and Sammy Cahn:

> "Love and marriage,
>
> Love and marriage
>
> Goes together like a horse and carriage
>
> This I tell you brother,
>
> You can't have one without the other."

There is this desire of God to have a deep and abiding relationship with His people. The words of the Lord spoken through the prophet Hosea go as follows:

> Behold, I will allure you to me, and I will speak kindly to you. I will bring hope into your life. Your spirits will be lifted up, and your life will become a living song to me. I will bring peace and contentment to your life, because I want to marry you and to stay married to you forever...yes I seek your hand in marriage to be my wife forever. I offer you a relationship built on righteousness, justice,
>
> loving-kindness, compassion, and faithfulness. Then you will know me and I will know you, and you will know just how much I love you!
>
> Hosea Chapter Two (Paraphrase by RLF)!

The writer spoke of God in romantic terms. The emphasis is upon the gentleness of God. This relationship will be built upon God's always doing the right thing and treating His people fairly with tenderness and compassion. He will always be faithful to His people and will never turn His back on them.

That word picture of the relationship that God desires to have with His people also describes how we should love our partner in life and how they ought to love us. If a relationship has these components, it will last until "death do us part."

Are there any of these components missing in your relationship?

8

A Kite Gone Bad

While sitting in my study at Mount Vernon Baptist Church, located in the community known as Vale, North Carolina, I was trying to come up with some activity that would involve the whole congregation. I can't remember where the thought came from, but it occurred to me that flying kites would be a neat activity to do. It was just the right time of the year, so why not give it a try.

So in my next church newsletter, I set the date of the event for the last Saturday in March. I was hoping the weather would be conducive to our activity and the warm spring air would be invigorating. Turned out I was right; it was an excellent day for flying kites with moderate temperatures and the March winds in full display.

I was pleasantly surprised at the number of our church family who turned out for the event. I asked the owners of a large field next to the church for permission to use their property. Although there were a few power lines here and there, the field offered the best location. The assortment of kites was amazing! Soon there were kites flying in all directions.

About 30 minutes into our activity, I noticed one of the kids in the center of the field with string from head to toe. Soon his cry for help echoed in all directions. You would have thought he was being eaten by some ungodly creature. From a distance, it was difficult to determine the identity of the child in distress, but a closer examination revealed that it was Nathan Heavner. The poor kid was totally immobilized. There was no escape! He needed help.

So as we gathered around him trying to figure out this maze of string and kite. We decided to take the easy way out by just cutting him free. The incident reminded me of a Carl Shultz cartoon with Charlie Brown in a similar situation. Charlie Brown on his annual attempt to fly a kite was seen running this way and then that way, with the final frame having him wrapped from head to toe in kite string and kite. He, too, had become immobilized.

How easy is it to get our lives wrapped around us so tightly that we can't respond to the changing world. So easy to get caught up on our world and not be able to experience the greater world that surrounds us. While we don't always see the entrapments that plague a portion of our population, we can rest assured they exist.

In his book, *A Black Theology of Liberation*, James H. Cone says liberation theology is the heart and soul of Biblical theology. The theme that permeates the scriptures from Genesis to Revelation is liberation. God is about the business of liberating His people from the confining restraints placed upon their lives. The place to which God seeks to bring His people is the place of freedom: free to live and discover who we are and our calling in the world around us.

It is in this perspective Cone understood the scripture: "Come unto me all you who are bound by strings and kites, and I will give you freedom. Take my restraints upon you and learn of me; for my restraints are easy and my calling for you will be like a breath of fresh air." Matthew 11:28 (Paraphrase by RLF)

In the same sense, the beatitudes from the Sermon on the Mount should be seen in this light. "Blessed are the poor in spirit (those who have given their lives away, that is, emptied their lives in order that others may have life) for their life will be filled with the gift of God." Matthew 5: 3 (Paraphrase by RLF)

Becoming liberated, one then becomes a liberator. Only the person who has been liberated can give his/her life away in the removal of the proverbial "strings and kites" that are attached to many a life.

In the temptations of Jesus, the adversary was not offering freedom and fulfillment to Him, but the restraints of power, popularity, and fortune. It is one thing to own something; it is another thing for it to own us. There is a story of a rich young man (I'll make it clear, it's not a sin to be rich, but it is when we are owned by our riches.) who came to Jesus and wanted to become a disciple. Jesus said, "Sure, we could use a disciple or two more. Go and sell all you have and come follow me." We are told the young man went away sad, because he had many riches.

In contrast, when Zacchaeus, the chief tax collector (who became rich by cheating people from whom he collected taxes) met Jesus, he experienced a transformation. The winds of change that blew upon Zacchaeus that day directed him to give half of what he owned to the poor. To those he had cheated, he gave four times what he had stolen from them.

Both men were tied to their possessions, but only one was able to let go and become liberated. Truly, the person who is able to give his or her life away will find life, while those who keep their lives will lose them. Tied up? From what do you need to be liberated?

9

A Man Running After Me

Bit by bit he was catching up to me. How could I escape from this giant of a man just a few steps behind me? I was sure he would inflict pain and suffering upon me. It's not easy being a four-year-old in an adult world. I can't remember what I did that put me in this perilous situation, but I do remember the chase. As I made my way down the pathway that led into the woods, I felt a hand on my shoulder and then an arm around my waist. In spite of my best efforts, I had been caught. No way to wiggle myself out of this entrapment.

Before I knew it, I was in my father's arms as he carried me back to the house. After that, I draw a blank. I can't remember what happened that led up to the chase, but I remember the fear of being caught. Thus, the chase has lingered in my mind for all these many years. I don't recall doing that again, but I do remember it the first time around.

Yes, it was the cool of the day as He walked down the pathway looking for His children. Where could they be and why were they not answering Him? Two grown adults hid away in some bushes, afraid of being found. What was this intruder into their life going to do to with them? More important, why was He looking for them? Something deep inside of them knew why. Their imagination ran wild as they felt a sense of guilt and shame. But was it their fault? They had had help getting into the current situation. In fact, it had never entered their minds they were taking something that did not belonged to them. There was this influence that made them do it. If it had not been for this influence, they would have been okay. But still, they ran and ran and ran until they could run no more. The Hound of Heaven was after them and there was no getting away.

The Psalmist reflected on this as follows:

"Where can I go from Your Spirit?

Or where can I flee from Your presence?

If I ascend into heaven,

You are there;

If I make my bed in hell,

behold, You are there.

If I take wings of the morning,

And dwell in the uttermost parts of the sea,

Even there Your hand shall lead me,

And Your right hand shall hold me

If I say, 'Surely the darkness shall fall on me,'

Even the night shall be light about me;

Indeed, the darkness shall not hide [me] from You..."

Psalm 139: 7-12a (KJV)

The Psalmist was telling us about the futility of trying to run from God, because wherever we go, He is there. But there is a deeper issue here and that is our attempt to escape from our number one enemy. It is most difficult to escape this enemy that is in us and a part of us. It has been called our "alter ego." The dark side of who we are.

Thus, it is the task of facing up to ourselves and being willing to take a good look, not just on the outside, but going deeper into the Holy of Holies of our lives. It is a journey into our inner souls, and it is all about discovering who we are in light of the presence of God who pursues us and will not leave us alone and will not give up on us.

On every January 6 of the year, we enter the season of Epiphany. It is a season of discovery, discovering the deeper presence of God in our lives and His ongoing activity. It is discovering that what we have gone looking for in the world during the Advent Season (Christmas) to make our life more meaningful is already with us and within us.

As my father chased after me, seeking to embrace me and bring me back home where I belonged, so has God chased after me because He cares for me and loves me. He has never given up on me or forsaken me to my own will and ways. He has always been my Hound of Heaven even when I didn't know that I had one.

Psalms 46:10 tells us what we need to do "Be still, and know that the 'I Am.' [God] has drawn near to us and has embraced us." (Paraphrase by RLF)

From what are you running?

10

A Pointing Finger

Revival! Revival! Revival! The big event of the summer was coming to Big Level Baptist Church, a small rural church in Polk County, North Carolina. For the first time, circumstances of life had made it necessary for me to spend that summer on my grandparents' farm, so this was an event I had never experienced. There was no air conditioning in the church, so all the windows were wide open and the complimentary hand-held fans, which were provided by the local funeral home, were all in constant motion. Most of the men sat near an open window so they could spit their tobacco juice outside. Young mothers breastfed their babies with a sense of pride and at times with very little discreetness.

Prior to the service, the visiting evangelist made his way through the congregation making sure to hug the women and kiss the babies. He seemed to be well known by everyone and well-liked by all. He was a short, thin man, probably not weighing more than 150 pounds. He had a very serious look on his face which in some way was a prelude to his sermon. He wore a white shirt with the sleeves rolled up to his elbows. Like a starting baseball pitcher, he was ready to go to the "pitcher's mound" (pulpit) and deliver the Word of God to a lost and sinful people.

Eventually, it came time for the sermon, and the Reverend Griswold stepped up into the pulpit. What had seemed to be a mild-mannered man was now laid aside. Something happened at this time which was hard to describe. This mild-mannered man became a ball of fire. His voice resonated throughout the congregation, no need for a microphone or a sound system. How this loud sound came out of such a small man is a mystery. He moved with great speed from one place to another on the platform and eventually made his way up and down the center aisle. Up and down the aisle he would go, swinging one of the longest index fingers I had seen in my young life. At times it seemed he was pointing it right at me.

He was very animated in his delivery, as he transformed himself into the various Biblical characters of which he spoke. He seemed to quite enjoy this lively style with the folks. There was a glass of water on the pulpit, from which he would drink at times during the sermon. He spoke so rapidly it was difficult to keep up with him. His animation throughout his delivery brought real life to these Biblical characters portrayed in his sermon. In a sort of way, he took on their character as his own. It led me to believe he was not a man to be trifled with, once he started delivering the sermon.

Thank God, I sat between my grandparents! I knew they would protect me from whatever this man was threatening us with. Although I can't remember what the sermon was about, I can imagine it had something to do with "hell fire and damnation." which I knew very little about. To say the least, it was an experience not easily forgotten.

Looking back, I had some idea of how the congregation in New England must have felt during Jonathan Edwards' electrifying sermon, "Sinners in the Hands of an Angry God." The God the Reverend Griswold brought to us that night was very angry with us, and we were in danger of being sent some place we would not want to go.

In fact, when the invitation was given at the end of his sermon, there was a mass movement of people coming forward to receive assurance the threat of damnation would not happen to them. I'll have to say, I felt a need to go forward in spite of not knowing what the threat was all about, but for whatever reason, I decided to stay put.

The bottom line is we have some accountability in life. The comedian Flip Wilson always said the devil made him do it. In other words, it was always someone else who caused him to act in a bad way. I often see this carried out on the Judge Judy Show. Everyone seems to tell his/ her story with a certain slant toward someone else's being responsible.

Karl Menninger, M.D., founder of the Menninger Foundation and Clinic located in Topeka, Kansas, wrote in his book *Whatever Became of Sin?* that the disappearance of the notion "SIN" has been a process in which more and more the popular opinion of the culture defines what is right and wrong. In other words, the voice of the church seems to be less and less audible.

So many loud voices drown out the "still small voice in the wilderness" that seeks to bring guidance and direction to our lives. We are reminded that out of stillness come the creative acts of God, and out of silence, God speaks. This seems to be a problem! We can't be quiet, and we can't be still.

In his conversation with his people, Moses directed his words to the tribes who didn't want to cross over the Jordan River into the Promised Land. He said to them: "Take note, if you do not go with us, you sin against God, and your sins will find you out." Numbers 32: 23 (Paraphrase by RLF)!

We are often reminded we only go through this world one time, so we need to get all the gusto we can get. To say it another way: "Eat, drink, and be merry for tomorrow you may die." It's amazing that a lot of people thought the end of the world was coming with the turn of the century. Credit cards were maxed out, thinking the end would come before the bill.

Yes, the Reverend Griswold with his long index finger pointing out at the congregation that hot summer night reminded us that "I" is in the middle of "S – I – N". As the song goes, "It's not my brother or sister, but it's me, O Lord, standing in the need of prayer."

Who's pointing a finger at you?

11

A Tough Shot to Handle

I was minding my own business sitting in my office at work when the phone rang. On the other end was someone from Operations Headquarters, Department of the Army, "Is this Colonel Ford?"

"Yes, speaking!"

"We have orders for you to deploy to Kuwait. Are you willing to accept these orders?"

"Yes sir, I am!"

"You have 30 days to be at the processing unit at Fort Benning, Georgia. Thank you, and have a good day."

The conversation was short and sweet, but it had left me stunned. Of all the phone calls I might have gotten that day, this was not one I expected. It had been just over a month since the U.S. invaded Iraq, so I was not expecting to get a phone call like that so soon. I remained in my chair, leaned back and closed my eyes. I had to take a few moments to process this. Tears started to build up in my eyes and overflowed, running down my cheeks and along the corner of my mouth before continuing their journey down my neck. I hated the thoughts of leaving my family!

I had always been up front with my family that if I were ever called up, I would go. It wasn't fair for me to play it safe and stay at home, while thousands of other soldiers were called up. It was a promise I had made, and I was going to stick with it. Although I had been in a similar situation in the Air Force, then I did not have a wife and child to leave behind. This time it was different!

During my preparations to leave, I received another phone call from the Department of Operations telling me my orders were being changed to Germany. I would be part of a back-fill for the First Armored Division. It seemed the First Armored Division was the first to hit the ground in Iraq, so I would be going to Germany with 50 chaplains and chaplain assistants to provide coverage for the staff and families left behind. My report date had been moved up to mid-June. That was great—our wedding anniversary and my wife's birthday fall right into that time frame.

In mid-June I was at Fort Benning, Georgia. The in-processing procedure was almost like going into service for the first time. There was paperwork to fill out that seemed to be a mile high, and medical exams kept me busy about all day. Then came the time for shots! Our shot records had to be up to date. Then came the biggie! The shot of all shots – Anthrax! The person administering the shot explained what it would feel like and what to expect. The information wasn't good.

It would sting at point of contact and then it would spread like wildfire all over the body. I would feel cramps and cold sweats as my body reacted to the invasion. I would think I was having a heart attack. The pain would continue to intensify for 30 minutes. The attendant would stay with me in case other medical help was needed.

"Do you have any questions?"

"Yes, which way is the door?"

Well, I'll have to say, they didn't lie. It was as bad as or maybe even worse than presented, but I lived through it. "Oh yes, one more thing. Your whole body will be sore tomorrow. Now have a good day!"

"Yeah, sure thing!"

In addition to receiving the shot, I had been taught how to give myself a shot if I came into contact with poisonous gases. I thought it might be simpler just to lie down and die. But, now I was fully "bona fide!" I was ready to take on the world, that is, as soon as I recovered. It was an experience I would not soon forget, and certainly not one I would want to repeat. But I had no complaints. I was still walking and breathing, and, so far as I knew, I was still alive.

There is an old saying that keeps shooting through my mind. "No pain, no gain!" In order to give me the very best chance of living, I had to go through a very painful experience. There was no way of getting around it. It wasn't the first time I had had to endure pain in order to live a healthy prosperous life. At a young age I had my tonsils and adenoids taken out. That left me speechless for a while, and with a very sore throat. In more recent times, my dentist found some suspicious looking spots on my tongue that an oral surgeon later removed. I couldn't eat correctly for more than a year, and lost about 20 pounds. Not the way that I would want to lose weight!

It is our nature to avoid pain at all cost, but there are times we cannot escape it. Pain is not an intrusion into life, but a part of life. We all have felt some form of pain in life. While it is hard to hide our physical pain, psychological pain wears many masks. Rather than claim it, we often stuff it deep down into our souls. There, it remains hidden from the world and from us as well. Later on, we wonder why we feel bad all the time. We gain weight! We lose weight! We have more headaches and back pain and wonder where it is coming from.

Isaiah 53 painted a picture of the Jewish nation in exile and their eventual homecoming. It would be a painful journey. Isaiah wrote: "This report, about God's chosen people, is a hard one to believe. Has the work of the Lord been revealed to anybody? God's only child (Israel)! His chosen nation shall grow as a tender plant. It will be born out of a most desperate situation. Its body will be deformed and ugly. There will be no beauty to make it desirable. Instead, the child will be despised and rejected. When the child takes on manhood, the world will say of him: "He is a man of sorrows who bears a load of grief."

Let us hide from him; least his countenance consume us. We despised him. We would not allow him to have his proper place in our life. In a most mysterious way, he has carried our burden of grief and sorrow. Yet, we saw him as worthless; a person punished by God with afflictions. He carried our transgressions upon his shoulders. He was beaten and bruised for our immoral behavior. We enjoyed peace at his expense. His punishment allowed us to heal and feel the wholeness of God." Isaiah 53: 1-6 (Paraphrase by RLF).

The above scripture is often thought of as describing an individual from the nation of Israel, but it could just as well be a description of Israel as the special child of God. Through their suffering and hardships comes forth the Word of God. It is in the New Testament that this image is narrowed down to an individual, Jesus of Nazareth. It is through his life of suffering and pain that the revelation of God the Father shines through and fills the earth.

Pain in itself does not heal! It is the act of laying claim to our pain that brings the possibility of healing. We may stuff our pain deep down into our souls, or we may embrace our pain. Embracing our pain means we take ownership of it. It belongs to us. What has happened has happened! While we cannot change our past, we can make changes in the present moment. In the right now of life, we can make changes that will allow healing of our mind, body, and soul.

I love the book by Henri Nouwen, *The Wounded Healer*, which so effectively describes how we may become a healing presence in our world through our own pain and suffering. In fact, the one thing that connects the whole world of humanity is that we all have been wounded.

Perhaps then, we ought to pray not for a life free from pain but for the courage to embrace the shot of pain life brings our way and to be transformed by it.

It is through this process of transformation that the new creature in us begins to rise to the surface of our lives. It is this new life that empowers us to be a healing presence. So, some of what God accomplished through Israel, and later on, through the historical Jesus, He now accomplishes through us.

We are God's healing agent in our world of pain and suffering. If we are willing to accept this "Mission Possible," we, too, may be exposed to much suffering and pain. That is the hidden meaning of the commandment to "Take up your cross and follow your Lord."

Are you up for this journey?

12

Abandoned

He looked a lot like Buddy Holly, a former rock-and-roll singer from the late 50s, and oddly, too, his name was Buddy. He was a young minister, perhaps in his mid- to late-twenties, who was at his first pastorate. Before he could even get his feet wet in this new environment, he was drawn into a church conflict that had been brewing for years. It seemed a certain Sunday School teacher was not using the proper literature in her class. Some members of the deacon board came to the Reverend Buddy Oliver to find a solution to this ongoing problem. They wanted her to be relieved of her teaching duties, but they were not sure of the best way to go about this delicate task. When the nominating committee met to discuss the matter, they decided she needed to be replaced. Being that he had the backing of the deacon board and the nominating committee, the Reverend Oliver agreed to go along with their decision.

The report was given in a church business conference, and the teacher in question stood up and pleaded for her teaching position. She said teaching was what gave her life meaning and purpose. At that moment, the whole issue became the reverend's fault. It was the preacher who had done this. Yes, the young minister found himself in a position that made him the scapegoat for the deacon board and the nominating committee.

After the incident, Reverend Oliver's ministry at that church had no chance of survival. It became very obvious; he needed to move on to another church. The abandonment of the deacon board and the nominating committee had taken the wind out of his sails. So, he decided since things had not worked out for him in the western foothills of North Carolina, he would try again in the eastern coastal section of the state.

Here, he could put the bad experience behind him and go on with his ministry as planned. So, he took a pastorate in a small coastal community. The major issue folks faced there was hurricanes. When a hurricane came up the east coast, folks had to decide whether to leave or stay. At some point, the road and bridge leading to and from the community would become flooded. Once that happened, there was no getting in or out of the community.

Since the church was located on higher ground, some of the concerned members came to Reverend Oliver with a proposal that the church fellowship hall be used for folks who decided to stay on the island when a hurricane came through. The minister and the deacons of the church would be there to give assistance.

It was not long after the meeting that a hurricane came roaring up the eastern coast. As it became more and more evident the hurricane would strike this community, the minister began to call his deacons. He soon discovered they were no longer on the island. They had left the area long before the road and bridge were flooded. The minister and his family were stuck on the island with no way to get off.

Indeed, the hurricane came and blew its winds upon the small community. The minister and his family gathered in the hallway of the parsonage to wait out this category four hurricane. At times, it sounded as though the whole house would just blow away. In his mind, the minister knew they were going to die. It was just a matter of time! Eventually, the noise of the wind and rain went away. Nothing could be heard from the outside, so the Reverend Oliver decided to go outside and check things out.

Outside, he looked up and saw blue sky and a few white clouds. The land below them was flooded, but water had not reached the parsonage or the church. He knew they had dodged a bullet. They were still alive and that was all that mattered. Standing on his front porch, he began to feel the wind coming from the opposite direction. At first just a gentle breeze, and then he could hear the storm coming again. He realized then that the storm had not passed, but the leading edge had come through, and it was the eye of the storm that deceived him.

The Oliver family survived the storm. A lot of damage was left in the wake of the storm, but the important thing was, his family was safe and sound. As he thought through what had transpired and what had happened to the plans to make the church fellowship hall a place of refuge, Reverend Oliver realized his church had abandoned him again. No one called him about the change of plans. The deacons left the island without informing him the plans were off. The abandonment had taken away his enthusiasm for the work of ministry in that community, so eventually he moved on to another denomination and church in Tennessee.

I find Reverend Oliver's life situation to have some similarity to that of Uriah who was a soldier in King David's army. Uriah's life unfolded in Second Samuel 11: 6 – 17. While he was away fighting in a war with the Philistines, his wife was back home sunbathing atop their city dwelling. For some reason, King David chose not to participate in this war and turned his responsibilities over to his field commanders. While taking a leisurely stroll out on his upper patio and surveying the area that surrounded his palace, he noticed a young lady sunbathing in the nude. Instead of just noticing her, he allowed his gaze to last for a long time. Finally, King David had one of his servants go and escort the woman to him. Upon her arrival, she was taken to his bedroom. There he made love to her, and she became pregnant with his child.

Upon learning the woman he was having an affair with was pregnant; King David pondered how to shift the blame to someone else. The woman's name was Bathsheba and her husband was Uriah. David sent a note to his top commander to let Uriah come home for some rest and relaxation (R&R), but upon arrival, Uriah refused to go into his home to be with his wife. He refused to enjoy the comforts of home while his men were still out on the battlefield.

So King David sent Uriah back into battle with a note to give to Joab, his top commander, to place Uriah on the frontlines of the battle and then to withdraw all the troops. Alone on the battlefield, there was no hope for Uriah to survive. The challenge was too great for Uriah to overcome, and he soon lay dead upon the battlefield. He had been betrayed by the one person he thought would always do the right thing. His loyalty to King David was without flaw. There was nothing he would not have done for the commander-in-chief, but unfortunately his king did not have the same loyalty to Uriah. Uriah was abandoned!

The Gospel according to Matthew gives an account of the crucifixion of Jesus. Matthew tells us, Jesus died alone. All of his family and friends, including his disciples, had abandoned him. At 3:00 on Friday afternoon, Matthew recorded the final words of Jesus: "My God, my God, why have you forsaken me?" Matthew 27: 46c (Paraphrase by RLF).

Abandonment is not something we do to ourselves; it is something that is done to us. While others may forsake us, the scriptures remind us "God will never forsake us or leave us." Although there are times that like the historical Jesus we feel as though God has forsaken us, He has not. God is always where He needs to be no matter how we feel. So, when we need Him the most, we can rest assured, He is present.

In the Book of Kings (I Kings 18), we find Elijah running for his life. On Mount Carmel, not far away, he had conducted the slaughter of 450 priests representing the worship of Baal. It so happened King Ahab's wife was of that denomination. When she heard what Elijah had done, she swore to have Elijah killed the next day. So he decided to hide in a cave. In his aloneness, he felt God had abandoned him. From the cave, he heard thunder and lightning, wind and rain, but there was no comfort for him. Then, things outside quieted down, and a silence filled the cave. It was in the midst of this silence that he was able to hear the "still small voice of God," which called out to him. This encounter changed his life and empowered him to leave the safety of the cave and to follow his calling.

Heard any "still small voices," lately?

13

Basic Training

It was late afternoon as we traveled from the military induction center in Charlotte, North Carolina. We had passed all the tests, received all our shots, and taken the oath of enlistment. Now, we were on our way to our basic training post in San Antonio, Texas. We soon discovered a major part of our daily routine at Lackland Air Force Base (AFB) was physical training (PT). Along with sit-ups and push-ups, we were required to do several laps around the half-mile track. Since there were so many of us, we were divided into groups of 50. Each group took its turn while the rest of us waited, standing at attention. The difficult thing about standing at attention is you are not supposed to move at all; I mean not even to blink an eye or wiggle your nose, even if a fly lands on it. So, there we were standing in the infield waiting our turn to run around the track four times.

The PT instructor was Paul Anderson, former gold medalist at the 1956 Olympics in weight-lifting. This was the Year of Our Lord, 1965, and the man was still in great shape. I don't know if it were true or not, but from the high stand he was on, he called out that somebody had moved. He asked that person to come forward. Several seconds went by, and no one made a move to go forward.

Then, he got a little more specific about what was going to happen if that person did not come forward. Believing I had not moved, I stood my ground, but more than 150 basic trainees saw fit to go to the front. I thought I was going to be trampled to death during their movement forward, but I survived. The punishment was they had to do an additional two laps around the track. Those of us who stayed back were watched like hawks. There was only a dozen or so of us, so the training instructors (TIs) continued to walk back and forth in front of us to ensure there was no movement. Man, I was sweating bullets!

You might think those instructors were being mean and cruel to us, but that was not their intent. Their intent was to save our lives, because obeying orders in the military can be a life-or- death matter. Knowing when to move and not to move and staying down are highly important. All of this requires discipline on the part of the soldier. This is what basic training in all branches of service is about. Knowing and carrying out orders is what makes it all work.

I believe the Apostle Paul would have made a great TI in any branch of service. In First Corinthians 9, Paul wrote about how one prepares to run a race and compares it to how one is to live the Christian life: "Know you not that they who run in a race run all; but only one receives the prize? So run, that you may obtain. Every person who strives for the mastery is temperate in all things. Now they do it to obtain a prize that has a short shelf-life, but we seek after a prize that will last forever. I, therefore, run with a great deal of certainty. I fight not as one who beats the air, but I keep under discipline my body, mind, and spirit, so that what I preach, I practice, and not be seen as a hypocrite." (Paraphrase by RLF)

What are you training to become?

14

Broken Bones

The sound of skates filled the room as 100 or more children, teenagers, and adults made their way around the rink. It was a Saturday morning at the local skating rink, which was crowded with folks having a variety of skating expertise. I was one in the group just a little above the beginners' group. After a couple of hours of perfecting my moves, I decided one more lap around the track and I would call it a day. As I was in the process of making my way to the rails to exit the main skating area, one of the skaters, trying to skate backwards, slammed into me. Since I was hit from the back, both my skates left the floor and I fell backward onto the hard floor. When I hit, I felt an enormous pain in my left arm. I soon discovered it was broken. My injury became apparent to everyone, and several skaters helped me up from the floor. The bone in my arm was protruding through the skin. as I tried to hold the whole thing together.

One of the skaters volunteered to drive me to the hospital. So off we went, both with our skates on. At the emergency room, we were making our way up a small ramp when I slipped and fell. My driver was helping me hold my arm together at the time, so when I fell, he stood there holding my hand while the rest of me was on the ground. I nearly passed out!

After the surgery, my parents were informed by the medical staff they had done the best they could do with my arm. It had been a compound fracture (both bones in my arm broken), and because the bones had splintered my arm would be a little crooked. I spent just over a week in the hospital, after which I was informed another team of doctors (specialists) were going to re-do the surgery and attempt to make my arm straight. It seemed Mom was not satisfied with her son having a crooked arm. So back to the operating room for the second time, but this time the surgery was successful.

At the end of my second week, I was discharged from the hospital with my arm in a cast. Since I'm left-handed, that made life a little difficult. I couldn't wait to get the cast off my arm so I could get back to a normal 14-year-old kid's life. When the doctors removed my cast, my arm just floated up into the air. It felt so light, but it was straight as an arrow. I took the cast and hung it on the wall in the shed behind our house. Over my teen years, I added many more casts to my collection.

Had my broken bones taught me anything? At the time, no! I still participated in activities that had some element of danger. I continued to roller skate, and play basketball and football on Sunday afternoons at Spartanburg Methodist College. I sprained both ankles and broke a bone in one of my ankles, knocked my left arm out of joint, and broke a finger playing softball. If those events were supposed to teach me something, it wasn't getting through to me.

In his book, *When Bad Things Happen to Good People*, Rabbi Harold S. Kushner wrote that sometimes there are no obvious reasons why things happen the way they do. Stated simply, the answer is there is no answer. The scripture says "The rain falls on the just and unjust." That means good things happen to all people and on the other side of this coin is that bad things happen to all people.

Broken bones like broken lives bring a great deal of pain into our lives. They demand our immediate attention. The brokenness that occurs in our lives may take many forms. In addition to a physical breakdown, there are psychological and spiritual breakdowns. More often the physical issues get immediate attention, while psychological and spiritual issues are often put off for another day. That is unfortunate, because healing of the soul (the total person) involves the body, mind, and spirit.

If the infection is allowed to fester in any of these areas, the healing process becomes more complicated.

Healing comes out of the area of life that is experiencing the most pain and suffering. Eventually, a condition known as hemostasis, which describes a level playing field, is reached and life returns to what is normal for us. As strange as it may sound, pain gives birth to life. Think of it: the place in a hospital where new life is brought into the world is called the "labor room."

So here's the deal. To deny your pain in any of the three areas of your life (mind, body, spirit) is to deny the total dimension of healing that is available to you. Rather than deny it, you need to embrace it. When you claim it, you are ready to do something with it. You are ready to be open to the resources in your family, church, and community. That is the process God uses most often to bring healing into our lives.

I would be remiss if I did not bring in the words of our Lord at this point: "Oh Jerusalem, Oh my children all over the world, how many times I wanted to bring you under my wings of healing, but you would not." Luke 13: 34 (Paraphrase by RLF).

In another place and time, Jesus asked those around him who were suffering in various ways, "Do you want to be healed?" It seemed like a question out of place, but in reality, he was asking, "Are you willing to participate in the healing I want to bring to you?" Think about it: when Jesus began the process of healing in someone, he would often tell them to go do a particular task to complete the healing process? By this, they were being asked to participate in the healing process.

What do we do with our brokenness? We may be a mister fixer-upper and attempt to heal ourselves, or we may allow ourselves to be open to the community God has placed around us. The choice is ours.

Are there any broken bones in your life?

15

Bucket Lists

There are certain plateaus in life that give rise to a variety of needs. It was the tender age of 70 that inspired me to look back over my life and determine what I always wanted to do but had never taken the time to do. I had tried out a Harley Davidson and that didn't work out too well for me, so what else could I do?

In college, I signed up for skiing lessons, which counted for one hour of credit toward my degree, but the weather did not provide the conditions for skiing. It seems the mountains of western North Carolina received a lot of rain, but very little snow that year. So instead of skiing, I tried ice skating, which left me sprawled out on the floor and then crawling back to the railing in order to have another go at it. Later on when I was deployed to Germany with the Army, I went on a skiing trip with about 30 youth from our post. I ended up snowboarding with 15 of them, and I soon discovered snowboarding was not my thing either.

So now at this crucial age in my life, I asked myself, "What's next?" The only thing that came to mind was that although I had been on a lot of skiing trips, I had never skied. With this bright idea in mind, I told my wife what I would like to do for my birthday—go skiing. We followed the "yellow brick road" (Interstate 40) to Gatlinburg, Tennessee. The next day, I was on the slopes in a skiing class. Like a lot of things of this nature, I made everybody else look good.

I learned more about falling than I did about skiing. I began to wonder, "Isn't there an easier way to die?" I decided bucket lists are not all they're cracked up to be. Maybe there's an easier way to live out my life that would be less painful and more productive.

Then I began to think of all the Biblical characters who had discovered something late in their lives. Abraham and Sarah were in their 70s and 80s when their first child was born. Moses was in his 80s when he led the Israelites out of Egypt. That is interesting! Two of the most prominent people in the Old Testament were way beyond 70 when they accomplished some great things in their lives.

So, with a lot of encouragement from my family and friends, I started out on the adventure of writing my first book. With the help of my college and seminary buddy, Dennis Hester, I finally finished the book, sent the manuscript in and out came *Behind Grandma's Apron Strings: Stories of God's Grace and Mercy*. I didn't realize I had it in me. There are a lot more opportunities available to us, if we are willing to get out of our comfort zones and give it a try. Draw a picture! Do some pottery! Take a photography class and see what happens. Get involved in some area of your community. Help a neighbor, and then another and another. Well, you get the picture. Retirement is not about collecting dust until we die, but finding new ways life may still be very useful and rewarding.

What's on your Bucket List?

16

Caught in the Act

It was a very hot spring day, and we were trapped for at least an hour in Mrs. Collins' English class. Her 11 o'clock class was right before lunch, so thoughts of food seemed to prevail on most minds in the room. It was one of those times when it seemed the day would never end, and staying awake was a difficult thing to do. There was no air conditioning in the building, so our ground-floor classroom windows were wide open to allow an occasional breeze to pass through. A quick glance around the room exposed you to the boredom that had settled in.

Then the unexpected happened, which made you forget all the bad stuff that was going on. From my position, I could see James Cody coming up the walkway with some items in his hands. As he approached the building entrance, all of a sudden he disappeared. I soon discovered James had gotten down on his hands and knees and was crawling just below the windows. As he made his way along the side of the building, Mrs. Collins made her way to the blackboard near the windows. Her eye caught James as he continued his journey down the row of windows. Without a word, she slowly followed him. Soon James reached his destination, where Eldon Holt was sitting. James placed the items, which included a candy bar, on the windowsill. Having completed his mission, he glanced up to discover Mrs. Collins was looking down at him. She had caught him dead in his tracks. James immediately made a U-turn and continued to crawl back to the walkway, where he stood up and ran off toward the gym. When questioned by Mrs. Collins, Eldon denied any involvement in what had just transpired.

James and Eldon thought they could pull a fast one on Mrs. Collins, but it was Mrs. Collins who pulled a fast one on them. In the end, I don't think she took any action such as having the boys sent to the principal's office. In effect, there were no repercussions for their actions except for the embarrassment of being caught.

I suppose the most devastating thing for Eldon and James was the fact they had been discovered. In the Book of Genesis, we find the story of Adam and Eve, who thought they could sneak an apple off the forbidden tree. They thought no one would see them, but someone did. Feeling like they needed to do something, they ran and hid in some bushes. Ah, it was a good place to hide; no one would ever find them there.

They soon realized someone was walking through the garden looking for them. So, they remained quiet and still with the hope that the person would go away. That didn't happen! Instead, they heard a voice addressing them. "What are you doing? Why are you hiding in those bushes?"

They soon realized the voice was the voice of God, and He had discovered their hiding place. They felt afraid and vulnerable before Him. Not knowing what was going to happen, they did what we always do; blame someone else for our actions. It didn't work! They had to take ownership of their actions and the consequences as well. That was turning out to be a bad day for them.

One of the consequences was they had lost their innocence. They would never get that back. Then, they knew they were naked. They felt ashamed of their nakedness. There was a feeling of vulnerability. What would happen to them now? They had been caught! There was no place to run or hide?

Adam and Eve had to leave their home in the garden and find a new place to live. In the new place, they needed to work in order to carve out a living. But work is not a bad thing; it is an act of being a part of the process of creation. We all are co-creators with God. His creation finds fullness in His people and the good work they accomplish.

So, getting caught is not always a bad thing! It allows us to experience forgiveness, grace, and mercy and to discover a bad start does not necessarily mean a bad ending.

Have you been caught yet?

17

Do You Have a Light?

It was my first time doing this, so I was anxious and very much afraid of getting caught. The small convenience store on the corner sold me what I wanted, but would I get caught doing it? If my parents found out about it, I would be in big trouble! Well, I didn't want to be an odd ball. Anyway, a 14-year-old should have a little freedom about things like this. After all, wasn't this a part of growing up? So, I made my decision. I would go the store, put my money down on the counter with no questions asked. I had seen my father and both grandfathers use this product, so why couldn't I?

In a small field behind my house, I opened the package for the very first time. I knew the product was for adults only. There was excitement in just having the product in my hand; at looking at the neat container it came in and slowly moving my fingers down one side and up the other. I knew the whole thing was off limits for me, but that didn't matter now. I had crossed the point of no return. The gravitational force in the direction of the product was too much for me to overcome; I had to complete the process.

Slowly, I took a small box of matches from my pocket. I took one match and struck it against the side of the box, and right away it lit. I took one of the items from the other box and put it in my mouth. Once more, I looked in all directions to ensure no one in the whole wide world was looking, and then I held the burning match to the end of the long round Winston cigarette and breathed in. It was an electrifying experience! I coughed and choked for nearly 15 or 20 minutes. Did I listen to my body language? No! Not at all! I tried it again with the same results! You would think at some point I would have realized this was not good for me, but that never occurred to me at the time.

Eventually, my body accepted more than 1,000 different chemicals associated with cigarette smoking. In fact, my body accepted them so well, when I finally arrived in my mid-twenties, I discovered how difficult it was to quit. I tried to quit on several occasions but with little success.

During the course of my nearly 10-year history of smoking, I had been asked the question, "Do you have a light?"

My response would generally be, "Yes, I do!" I would then reach into my pocket, pull out a Zippo lighter and provide the needed fire to light a cigarette.

Fire is neither good nor bad; it is simply what it is—fire. At the end of a cigarette, it can cause a lot of health problems. In a fireplace, it can light up a room on a cold winter's night, while providing much-needed heat. The important issue is the context in which the fire burns. In the Sermon on the Mount, Jesus told those around him: "You are the light that lights up the world. You are like a city set on a mountaintop that cannot be hid. People don't light a candle, and then put it in a closet. What would be the point of that? They would put it on a candlestick, so it would give off light to everyone in the house! Therefore, let your light shine before all people, so they may see God through your life!" Mathew 5: 14-16 (Paraphrase by RLF).

In the creation story found in the Book of Genesis, the writer informed us we are created "In the Image of God." God is light, so His light is within us. When we discover that, we don't hide it, we share it.

So, do you have a light?

18

Do You Want-A Dance?

Ronnie Dorsey was having a birthday party at his home and invited his class at school to attend. Almost everyone from our sixth-grade class at Ruth Elementary School would be there. At the party there would be music and dancing. Dancing was not my thing at the time, so at every request, I would say, "No, I don't think so." Soon it became apparent to my classmates that I was the only one not on the dance floor. I became a classroom project. It became apparent to me the pressure from my classmates would not go away until I made my way to the dance floor. There was no getting out of this dance thing!

So, with some tugging from my classmates, there I was on the dance floor. Okay, all I had to do was what everybody else was doing. It shouldn't have been too difficult, but for me it was like a tooth being pulled without Novocaine. I made some moves, but always felt I was out of step with everyone else.

When my family moved to Spartanburg, South Carolina, in the fall of 1957, I attended Fairforest Junior High. Well, wouldn't you know it? One of the popular events at school was the local "Sock Hop" at the Memorial Auditorium! So, once again I was challenged with this dance thing that I felt very uncomfortable doing. I went with some male friends, who were probably no better at dancing than I was. We looked for girls we knew, particularly girls we thought would say yes to our invitation to dance. It seemed to me there was not one girl there whom I felt comfortable going up to and asking for a dance. What if they didn't know any more than I did about dancing? It would be like the blind leading the blind.

Finally, a girl from my school came over and asked me to dance with her. She was an attractive seventh grader, and I wondered why in the world this girl was asking me to dance? How could I say no... that's the point, I couldn't. Lucky for me, she had chosen a slow dance for us, and I thought maybe I could handle that. I suppose I did okay. After the first dance, we talked and eventually got some refreshments and stayed together for the remainder of the evening. I had gotten out of my comfort zone and had made a new friend. Life was getting a lot better!

I have since discovered dancing has many dimensions. A friend of mine, Eva Helton, introduced me to a song that is often sung at her church. It is called, "Lord of the Dance." Sydney Carter wrote the lyrics in 1963. His remarks about the song are as follows:

"I see Christ as the incarnation of the piper who is calling us.

He dances that shape and pattern which is at the heart of our reality."

Some of the words of the song go like this:

"I danced in the morning when the world was begun,

And I danced in the moon and the stars and the sun,

And I came down from heaven and I danced on the earth.

Dance, then, wherever you may be;

I am the Lord of the Dance, said he.

And I'll lead you all wherever you may be,

And I'll lead you all in the dance, said he."

Carter's song brings emphasis to how life is a dance and how we dance with others and especially with God. Like any other activity in which we might participate, dancing has its risks. In the TV show, "Dancing with the Stars," some of the contestants have gotten some bruises and broken bones. To dance with someone is to put some trust in them to do the right thing when it comes to the various challenges of the dance.

In Michelangelo's painting on the celling of the Sistine Chapel depicting the Act of Creation of Adam (the Hebrew meaning of the word is mankind), he has God holding out His hand to Adam. In a broader sense, it depicts God holding out His hand to all of humanity. It is as if God is saying to Adam, "Do You Want to Dance?"

Well then, "Do you want to dance?"

19

Fighting with Bruce Cooper

It was recess at Ruth Elementary School in the small community of Ruth, North Carolina. Mrs. Logan's fourth-grade class had an hour to play ball, shoot marbles, or just talk with friends. While I am sketchy on the process that led up to my fight with Bruce Cooper, I still remember the fight. Somehow, I made Bruce angry with me, and he challenged me to a fist fight. Fighting had never been one of my strong points, but for whatever reason, I decided to take Bruce on that day. Being left-handed, I caught Bruce looking for me to hit him with my right hand, but I got him with my left.

My punch landed square on his nose and immediately Bruce started crying. I felt bad about what I had done to him. I told him I was sorry I had hit him, and I did not mean to hurt him. I took a look at his nose to make sure it was all right. No blood could be seen, so I told him he was going to be okay.

Then I did a selfish thing! I offered Bruce a dime if he would not tell the teacher what I had done to him. He agreed to that, so we walked back to class with my arm across his shoulders and his arm across mine. I had given away my last dime, but it felt good that I had made peace with Bruce. Our friendship had hit a bump in the road, but in spite of that, we remained the best of friends.

It is not a sin to be angry, but it is what we do with our anger that causes us problems. The scriptures give us some insight on how we ought to handle our anger:

"Do not let your mouth cause your flesh to sin." Ecclesiastes 5: (Paraphrase by RLF)

WALKING IN GRANDPA'S FOOTSTEPS: STORIES OF GOD'S GRACE AND MERCY

"Do not hasten in your spirit to be angry." Ecclesiastes 7:9 (Paraphrase by RLF)

"Be angry, and do not sin. Do not let the sun go down on your anger." Ephesians 4:6 (Paraphrase by RLF)

There are some things that happen in our lives that we need to let go of. We need not hold onto the bad things some person has done to us, like they were pieces of gold. Unresolved anger not only affects our well-being, but it also produces a negative energy around us, causing others to become infected. It can travel through a family like a wild fire.

The story of the feud between the Hatfield family and the McCoy family in the post-Civil War years is well documented. It started out with one member from each family having a dispute over something that happened in the war. It soon spread throughout both families. The end result was the two families hated each other deeply. Forgiveness and reconciliation were not a part the solution. They wanted revenge at any cost. Eventually the leader of the Hatfield family committed suicide, and the leader of the McCoy family became a Christian. But as far as the feud, there were no winners.

We seem to live in a world today that shoots first and asks questions later. It reveals a deep-seated anger and distrust that prevail in some areas of our society. It's like we are walking around with a bunch of people who are walking time-bombs. Road rage has become a common occurrence out on our highways. The question is not if this is going to happen, but when.

Somewhere along the way, we get caught in the middle. It becomes like the "Charge of the Lite Brigade.". It was during the Crimean War and the Battle of Balaclava on October 25, 1854, that the Charge of the Light Brigade took place. The initial plan was for the British to attack the retreating Russian artillery battery. But there was a breakdown in communications on that day, so instead of a retreating battery, they found themselves in a frontal assault on a well prepared brigade. As the poem of Alfred Lord Tennyson indicates, there were cannons to the left and to the right, as well as in front of them. It was a no-win situation for the British troops.

Fighting on any level shows signs of our depleted humanity. To be truly civilized means we are capable of living at peace with our neighbors on all levels. It means the ability to work together to build a better world. It means to allow the freedom of expression of ideas. It means accepting others without trying to make them in our image. It means to embrace differences we discover in others, for it is only by embracing them that we may have the opportunity of making a difference in their lives.

We need to claim what we feel such as our prejudices, hatred, and distrust of others who are different. The appropriate action might be to take the risk of getting to know them. When we do that, we often find a common ground on which to build a meaningful relationship. In his poem, "Mending Wall," Robert Frost stated there is something that does not like a wall, but in the end, good walls make good neighbors. From my point of view, every wall should have a door in which thoughts and ideas may pass through both ways. Walls without a door produce isolation! Doors are bridges!

Jesus was quoted as saying in the Book of Revelation, "I stand at the door and knock, if you will open the door I will come in and create a fellowship with you and you with me." (Paraphrase by RLF) It is about our willingness to open the doors of our lives to the stranger who knocks. If we do, we might be surprised how God is working through this person's life to bless our life.

Does your wall have a door?

20

Giving Your Life Away

Early on in my career at the hospital, the call went out that we needed blood. "Will you help?" The Red Cross bloodmobile would be parked near the emergency room ready to extract that life-giving fluid. I decided to have a go at it, so I signed on the dotted line and then sat in line waiting my turn to enter the bloodmobile.

On my dog-tags from the Air Force, I was listed as having O positive blood, but tests proved that was wrong, I was O negative. If the Air Force had given me blood, it would have caused some serious problems for me, perhaps death. Fortunately for me, I never needed blood while I was in the Air Force.

My O negative blood could be given to anyone and was often given to newborn babies. I soon learned there was a high demand for my blood type due to the blood shortage of O negative. I believe at that time the minimum period one had to wait between donations was around 60 days. Donations became a regular event for me. I felt very good about giving the gift of life.

Not everybody can give blood. There is a check list of places you've been, diseases you've had and your current state of health, which determines if you are allowed to be a donor. In addition to this group, there are a large number of people who are afraid of needles. They can't bear the thoughts of having someone stick a needle in their arm and draw blood. They would go down like the Titanic.

One day Jesus told his disciples, "Greater love has no person, than the person who gives his/her life for another." Life Givers, that's what we are called to be in this world! In another place and time, Jesus told his disciples, "The person who keeps his/her life will lose it, while the person who gives his/her life away will find it." I believe on several occasions, Jesus used the words, "Lay down your life for another." That is an act of submission to the needs of our neighbors, which Jesus identified as being the entire world of humanity.

In his book, *Foxe's Book of Martyrs*, John Foxe takes the reader through a litany of individuals who died because they would not conform to certain religious practices. Foxe wrote his book back in the 17th century as he described the state of affairs in England. Today, there are still places in the world where being anything other than the state religion will get you executed.

On TV, I often see players who wear an empty cross which identifies the pathway to the Father. The words ring out, "Take up your cross and follow me!" Salvation is by way of the cross. On the other hand, the Catholic church embraces the crucifix. This is the occupied cross. The historical Jesus is there on his throne. The message is one of sacrifice. It is often the message we don't want to hear and the lifestyle we have difficulty embracing.

One of the popular commercials on TV says we only go through this world one time, so we need to get all the gusto available to us. The emphasis is on the word "get." The emphasis of the cross is "give." Again the words ring out, "To whom much is given, much is required." Unfortunately, in some worship services, the emphasis of the message is strongly skewed in the direction of what has been given to us and not much on what is required of us.

Are you a "Life Giver" or a "Life Keeper"?

21

God Is Out to Get Me

On a particular visit at the hospital, I met a patient who was distressed about many things. He began to tell me his story as he went over a history of one problem after another. He reminded me of the song on the TV program "Hee Haw," which says, "If it weren't for bad luck, I'd have no luck at all." At one point he finally said, "I think God is out to get me."

My response was, "That kind of puzzles me. I wonder what the problem is with God."

In a somewhat surprised voice he asked, "What do you mean there's something wrong with God?"

"Well, you say God is out to get you, but you are still here among the living. My question is why hasn't God gotten you yet? Is it that He is not that good a shot and He keeps missing you; or is it that He has lost track of you and doesn't know where you are? If God is out to get you, why are you still here?"

"What do you think that means," he inquired?

"What do you think it means," was my response back to him.

"I don't know, I haven't thought much about that," he said.

"Neither have I. Maybe it's something you need to give some thought to. I'll come back tomorrow and see what you've come up with."

The patient quickly responded, "Yes, that will be fine, maybe I'll have an answer for you tomorrow."

On my follow-up visit, I found the patient's room empty. The charge nurse informed me the patient had been discharged earlier than had been planned. I regret I did not have the opportunity to have the follow-up visit. I wondered if he had given much thought to my question, "If God's out to get you, why are you still here?"

While I could not sit down and have a conversation with the former patient, I could wrestle with my own question, "Why am I still here? Is it all about being chaplain at the hospital, or is there more to my life than this?" I was unable to come up with a decent answer other than my role at the hospital. It was not until years later that I discovered the other pieces to the puzzle of my life which gave me a clue that God had a number of things in mind for me.

My problem has been a lack of confidence in myself. In spite of the things God has done in and through my life, I still find myself doubting my ability to accomplish whatever it is God wants from me. I see my past successes as flukes and not as reflections of my ability to accomplish great things for God. I, too, have a hard time answering the question, "Why am I still here?"

Those guys out in boats fishing and making a living for themselves and providing food for their families and the community may have answered the question with one word, "fishing." Jesus met up with them and challenged them to follow him and promised they would become fishers of men. I knew they did not have a clue what he meant by that, but for some reason, they believed him, put down their nets, and as the Gospel according to Mark put it, they immediately followed Jesus down a new pathway. It would be a journey full of surprises, challenges, trials and tribulations, and eventually death.

But, life is not all about the end, for it is much more about the journey. Jesus told his disciples worry would get them nowhere. In the Gospel according to Matthew, Jesus gave them a bit of advice: "Do not worry about tomorrow, for tomorrow will have worries of its own; focus on each day of your life, and tomorrow will take care of itself" Matthew 6: 34 (Paraphrase by RLF)

Every day God goes fishing, because He is out to get us. Not to destroy us but to encounter us in all of life's issues and circumstances. He is always seeking to guide us from where we are to where we need to be.

Is God out to get you?

22

Humpty the Egg

In a faraway land, there was a farm, and on the farm they raised chickens. The farmer sold its eggs to the various grocery stores and restaurants throughout the land. Unknown to a lot of people, all eggs are not the same. While most of the eggs harvested on that farm were just common eggs, every now and then there an exotic egg would come along. It would be much larger than the other eggs, and the shell would be much brighter than the common eggs. It was a unique egg and eventually would make its way to far away museums and be painted with gold and silver. People from around the world traveled great distances just to behold its beauty.

On a particular day on the farm, as the mother hen attempted to adjust her position on the nest of eggs beneath her, there was something very uncomfortable about one of the eggs. She stood up and inspected each egg and found one had a large hump on it. She named this egg, "Humpty the Egg." The mother hen knew right away that Humpty the Egg was destined to become an exotic egg. Eventually, he would have arms and legs, eyes and a mouth to go along with his ears.

Growing up, Humpty the Egg was reminded by his mother he was very special and he needed to be careful in his activities, because he could very easily become broken. But, Humpty the Egg threw caution to the wind. "I'm special," he would say. "Nothing can happen to me!" He never took seriously the special gifts that had been bestowed upon him. He acted as though his special place in the world was all about what he wanted for himself.

In the local town of Nottingham, England, there was a castle with a high wall that surrounded it. One day, Humpty the Egg decided to climb up a ladder leaning against the wall. At the top was a narrow

WALKING IN GRANDPA'S FOOTSTEPS: STORIES OF GOD'S GRACE AND MERCY

walkway. His family and friends pleaded with him to come down, but he refused. He mocked them as he danced around on top of the wall. Their pleas to be careful were ignored.

At some time in every life there comes the unexpected! Something comes along we have not planned for, and it throws our life into a downward spiral. Such was the case for Humpty the Egg. Unknown to him, there was a small ground squirrel at the bottom of the wall. In the sky above, there was an alert hawk. As the hawk made its way toward the squirrel, it zoomed right past Humpty the Egg and startled him.

Humpty the Egg lost his balance and fell to the ground. He was broken all over his body. Everyone rushed in to help put him back together again. Eventually, special people, who are trained to deal with such situations, came to help. When all the pieces were put back in place and after Humpty the Egg had gone through extensive therapy, he was discharged from the hospital.

Back home, he stood in front of a full length mirror and observed the scars that now covered his body. A lot of his beauty was gone! In his mind, he was an ugly egg, not good for anything. In his world, there was so much emphasis on being pretty and beautiful, so how could he ever show his face again? His mind was made up; he would isolate himself from the rest of the world. They would never know how ugly he was with all the scars on his body.

One day, while looking out his window, he saw a man walking by who had lost part of his leg, and it seemed he was also missing part of one arm. In spite of that, the man was laughing and enjoying himself with his friends. For a leg, the man had some metal device connected to his leg that allowed him to walk. He also had some metal device connected to his arm that allowed him to hold things. Humpty the Egg was mystified as to how that man could do this.

So, Humpty the Egg opened his window and yelled out to the man, "May I have a word with you?"

The man turned, and seeing Humpty the Egg at the window, came over to him.

"Yes," said the man. "How may I help you?"

Humpty the Egg explained to the man about how he had fallen off the castle wall and had broken into hundreds of pieces and that he was ashamed to go outside anymore because of all his scars.

The man had been a soldier, and he had been wounded by an explosion that destroyed part of one leg and one arm. He explained that the best medical staff in the world had helped him learn to use his arm and leg. Although, that was not the way he wanted to be put back together, he was grateful for the opportunity to enjoy life, family, and friends. Sure he had lost a lot, but in spite of all the losses, he was still able to find a reason for living.

The soldier explained the spiritual transformation that had taken place in his life. At first his life was dark and gray. He wanted to die, not live! While he had given up on himself, his family and friends, and the medical staff had not given up. It was a slow process back to learning to walk and to use his arms. Looking back he now, though, he said the journey had been worth the effort. He now saw his life not as being handicapped but one full of possibilities.

Humpty the Egg was touched to his inner yoke. The life of this soldier challenged him to find the possibilities and potential for his life. He would wear his scars as a badge of courage and hope, not as a sign of defeat. For the first time in his life, Humpty the Egg discovered life was not all about him, but what he could bring to the world. His brokenness taught him a great lesson.

WALKING IN GRANDPA'S FOOTSTEPS: STORIES OF GOD'S GRACE AND MERCY

We may not get all we would like to have in life, and when we are broken, we may not be put back together as we were before. That does not mean our lives have no future. In fact, sometimes through our brokenness, we discover ourselves in new ways. Although this may not happen all the time, it does happen some of the time.

There is a story of a man and woman who experienced a great fall. Life had been as smooth as silk. Some would even say they had it made! As one knows, in every community there are some rules to live by. The landlord had a few rules about life in the housing development called "Paradise." It seems there was one particular fruit tree growing in the center of this community that was off limits to everyone.

You know how tempting it is when you see a sign on a park bench that reads, "Wet paint, don't touch!" You also know, eventually someone is going to touch it just to see if it is wet or not. So, as fate would have it, the young married couple decided to see what was so special about this forbidden fruit tree. They took fruit, and both took a bite.

The results were instantaneous! They were ashamed of what they had done and what they had become, so they ran away to a far place in the land. They could not face up to themselves or anyone else in the world. They felt they were the biggest losers in the world, and no one would want to have anything to do with them.

It does matter how we view ourselves and how we value ourselves, for this determines how we function in the world. The dark secrets we keep hidden deep down in the recesses of our souls determine more about us than we know or realize. This shadow side of our lives attempts to speak to us through our dreams and visions that we so often ignore.

Failure in life is not the worst thing that can happen to us, but the isolation that often comes from not being open to family, friends, and other resources of healing may lead us into a world of depression and despair.

This is perhaps the worst thing that can happen. We wear the mask that says, "I'm okay," while beneath it we are anything but okay.

There is a book on the history of God that tells the story of his salvation for all mankind. That does not come about by sprinkling some magic dust on those who have been scarred by life. The healing comes about by claiming our brokenness and our responsibility to do something with it. It requires that we swallow our pride and become open to the healing that is available to us! Rest assured, if we do not seek, we will not find.

What are you doing with your brokenness?

23

I Was Lost!

It was the weekend of the annual end of the season sales at the mall. Not wanting to pass up on some good opportunities, my family was off to this wonderland of bargains. In one of the department stores, my wife was looking around the various clothes racks while keeping a close eye on our four-year-old daughter. Lauran had wandered around to the other side of one of the clothes racks, but still was in view of my wife's very watchful eye. At some point, Lauran looked around and didn't see us. Immediately, panic struck her! She had been left behind! She then came running around the clothes rack, and upon seeing us, she exclaimed, "I was lost! I was lost!" Her mother informed her she had not been lost. We knew exactly where she was all the time. But, in our daughter's mind, she was lost and that was that, no matter what anyone said.

In the Gospel according to Matthew, we have the following words of Jesus about the issue of being lost: "Come, let us reason together. If you have 100 sheep and one of them comes up missing, do you not leave the 99 and go looking for the one that has gone astray? And when the sheep is found, you will rejoice!" Matthew 18: 12-13 (Paraphrase by RLF)

Amy-Jill Levine, professor of New Testament at Vanderbilt Divinity School, who happens to be of the Jewish faith, wrote about the above scripture in her book, *Short Stories by Jesus*. From a Jewish perspective, there had to be something very special about this one sheep for the shepherd to leave the other 99 unattended. In looking for the one sheep that was lost, the shepherd risked losing the 99. So, in spite of this risk, the shepherd left the 99 and looked for the one that was missing. In his mind, it was worth the risk. This particular sheep that was missing is one sheep that he could not live without. He must find it, because his life would not be the same without it.

When taken from this perspective, the story confronts us with the question, "What have you lost from your life that you would be willing to risk everything to find? What have you lost from your life that you can't live without?"

In the Book of Revelation, our Lord is described as standing at a door, knocking, knocking, and knocking, calling out, "I'm lost, open your door and find me." [Paraphrase by RLF] From that perspective, He is the one who is lost from our life, and we are challenged to take the risk of opening the door and find that which we can't live without.

Unfortunately, a lot of folks don't know they are missing anything. Sometimes it takes special times in our life to bring us to the realization we are missing something. In the beginning, we might not have a clue as to what it is, but if we are willing to do some soul-searching, we may come up with the answer. The discovery of what is missing must come from within us.

Jesus told a story of a man who walked back and forth across a field each day to get to and from work. He crossed the field for years, but one particular day he made a discovery that led him to go and sell everything he had in order to buy the field. What he found had been there all the time. He had just never seen it before. But he recognized the value of his find and knew deep down it was well worth the cost.

Finding the One who brings the presence of God into our lives is indeed a very valuable discovery.

The words of the song "Amazing Grace" echo this thought. I once was lost, but now I'm found. Was blind, but now I see! I have found what I can't live without!

Have you made that discovery?

24

Deep-Sea Fishing

I'm not sure whose idea it was, but it sounded good to me. Some of the men at my church had decided to go deep-sea fishing. I had tried fishing on many occasions, but with little or no success. On one particular trip to Lake Greenwood, I sat at the end of a pier with a shed built over it between two older ladies who were catching fish left and right. I was using the same bait they were using, and dropping my line to the same depth and still never got a bite.

So the opportunity to go deep-sea fishing was right up my alley. If I couldn't catch something out of the ocean, then I needed to just give up this sport of fishing. Our trip took us from Spartanburg to Murrell's Inlet, South Carolina. Boredom had settled in on our merry band of fishermen, so Harold Smith, Sr., decided to run through some high grass on the side of the road to see what kind of response he would get from the group. Charlie Blaylock was riding shotgun and was fast asleep. When our van hit the high grass, we thought Charlie was going to have a heart attack. It scared him, but it also made him mad that Harold would do such thing. From that point on, there was no more stunts by our driver, so eventually we arrived safe and sound at our destination.

We took a fishing boat out of Murrell's Inlet, located 15 or 20 miles south of Myrtle Beach. This was a favorite launching site for a lot of would-be fishermen who planned a 30-mile trip out into the Atlantic Ocean. On this day, our boat came slowly to a halt, and we saw the signal that it was time to put our fishing lines into the water. Periodically, the boat would rock from side to side and at times nearly dip us into the water.

WALKING IN GRANDPA'S FOOTSTEPS: STORIES OF GOD'S GRACE AND MERCY

An assortment of fish and other things were caught, and we were not sure what to call some of them. My best catch of the day was a red snapper, which weighed in at seven or eight pounds. It was so beautiful that I felt bad that I had caught it. At the end of the day, we all had our "nearly-caught-it stories."

One of our Baptist men became sick on our boat ride out to sea and spent the entire time in the hull of the boat. The movement of the boat became too much for Garland Martin, and he came down with what is called "motion sickness." The rest of us tried our best to hang on as the boat dipped one way and then another. In spite of all the boat movement, we were able to bring in a selection of fish and other sea creatures.

At the end of the day, we enjoyed a meal together and talked about what we nearly caught, as well as what we had actually caught. It was a good time with friends. It was also my first and last time on a deep-sea fishing trip, but it remains an experience that I am glad I had in life.

One day a group of men were fishing near the shores of Galilee without anything to show for their hard work. Frustration had set in and the men were about to call it a day, when a Voice from shore called out, "Put your nets over here." With some reluctance they obeyed the Voice. To their surprise, their nets were full, so full that additional help was needed to bring all the fish into shore.

"You have done well," said the Voice, "Now I will make you fishers of men. Throw your nets down and come follow me." Some believed and obeyed; others were reluctant and stayed back. Those who answered the Voice would fish for those who stayed behind. They were yet to realize that to become "fishers of humanity" they would need to become God's bait. God is doing the fishing, they will be the bait. As you know, it is the bait that gets eaten. Another form of giving your life away! Life is found in the catch. The catch becomes the source of new life. Give your life away and you find new life was Jesus' promise to his disciples.

We are called to allow the world at large to feast on us. What then is the nature of our bait-ness? What about us would draw the world to us? A fish goes for the bait because it is hungry. What is the world around us hungry for?

A song by Jackie de Shannon tells us that "what the world needs now is love, sweet love, there's just not enough of it." To be more specific, I would say it is "unconditional love" that draws the world of humanity to Christ and to those who follow him. If you want a better description go to First Corinthians Chapter 13. This is the kind of bait that the world of humanity is drawn to and desperately needs.

On our trip out to sea, we caught fish that we did not want, so we threw them back into the sea. When Jesus went fishing, he never threw any of the people he caught back into the fray. They were all keepers. He saw possibilities where other folks saw no possibilities at all. He saw what a person could be when he empowered them to achieve great things for God. For him, the lowest of humanity had potential to do great things for God. They were like nuggets in the rough. They had a hidden beauty that was not visible to the naked eye. But those who dared to see the world as God sees it also saw the hidden beauty of each and every person.

Through the record of his life and times, we see the world as Jesus saw it. He calls to us from the beggars on the street to those 100 floors above the street. No one is excluded. No one is thrown away as though they have neither value nor ability to make some contribution to life. The power of our witness will be seen in our willingness to embrace people as they are. Do not your goal be conversion or transformation, but acceptance. Learn how to accept people as they are. This is the nature of "unconditional love." This is the kind of bait that will attract those whom God is fishing for.

It had been a long day for Jesus as he finished up his sermon to the crowd of folks on a Galilean hillside. The next day found him in the community of Capernaum. There he was approached by some folks who had been looking for him from the other side of the lake, and wanted to know what had happened to him. Jesus cut to the chase and told them that their desire for him is more about having their bellies filled than to find nourishment for their soul.

He then described himself as the "divine bread" and said that those who want to satisfy their spiritual thirst must eat his flesh and drink his blood. This is a metaphor. He is the "Divine Bait" that will draw a multitude of people to him. "Feast upon me and you will know God."

So when Jesus calls us to be fishers of humanity, he calls us to be God's bait in the world. If we have feasted upon Christ, then we are walking with God. We can do this, because we are being transformed by that which we have taken into our being.

The greatest need of all humanity is acceptance. Accepting people as they are is the secret. This is the bait that draws them in.

Are you willing to be God's bait?

25

Mistaken Identity

It was the annual Halloween party at Skate Land USA for all the employees at Frye Regional Medical Center. Everyone was encouraged to dress up for the event. I believe my wife went as Kitty from the TV show "Gunsmoke," and I was dressed as Charlie Chaplin (a silent movie star). There was a contest for best outfit in the various categories of children, teenagers, and adults. Pizza and drinks were provided along with a lot of candy and cake.

Roller skating was optional! It was evident we had employees who were like Fred Astaire on skates and some more like Donald Duck on ice. All in all, it was a fun time for everyone! Of course, with a hospital of about 1,800-plus employees, there would be a lot of folks we did not know.

As my family was standing around taking a break from all the action going on around us, my wife attempted to make conversation with a lady standing near us. My wife's words went something like this, "I like your outfit! Thank goodness I'm not the only one wearing a costume tonight."

To this the lady replied, "I don't have on a costume."

Well, how do you get yourself out of something like that? It's not easy! I can't remember exactly how my wife did it, but it may have gone something like this, "Bless your heart. [This phrase is often used in the South to deal with a multitude of situations.] You look good anyway."

In the Old Testament there is a story of mistaken identity that had long-term effects. The story begins in Genesis 38 with one of Jacob's sons, Judah, who married and had three sons. The first son married, and before he could produce a child, he died. The custom of the day was for the next oldest son was to marry his brother's wife, which he did, but he refused to have children with her. Then, he died.

Judah made a promise to his son's wife, Tamar, that if she would go back and live with her parents until the third son grew up, he would give his third son to her as a husband. Tamar did that, but the years rolled by and she never heard from her father-in-law. The third son grew up, but was not given to Tamar as her husband.

Tamar came up with a plan. She heard through the grapevine that her father-in-law would be traveling through the area, so she put away her clothes of mourning and put on clothes that would identify her as a prostitute. She took her place by the side of the road and waited for Judah. Eventually, Judah came passing through the area and saw what he thought was a prostitute by the side of the road. He made her an offer of a goat that he would send to her later. She asked for collateral in the form of Judah's ring and staff which he gave to her. At that point, we know Judah was not the smartest man in the world.

Later on, when Judah tried to get his ring and staff back, the prostitute couldn't be found. Friends informed him his daughter-in-law had been seen playing the part of a prostitute. Judah ordered her to be stoned to death.

She was accosted by Judah's friends and brought before Judah, who ordered her execution. As that was about to happen, she pulled the ace out of her sleeve. Tamar revealed the ring and the staff that had been given to her by the man who got her pregnant. Judah immediately recognized the items as belonging to him. The next words he spoke were as follows: "She is in the right. I have failed in my obligation to her. I should have given her to my son in marriage." Genesis 38: 26 (Paraphrase by RLF)

Her pregnancy led to the birth of twin boys. One son was named Perez, and the other Zerah. They were children born out of a mistaken identity. You might think that would be the last time to see their names in print, but not so. Take a look at the genealogy of Jesus found in the first chapter of the Gospel according to Matthew. Read down a few lines and you see again the names of Perez and Zerah, and note their mother was Tamar.

Think about it. Here was a person abandoned by her family, abused by her father-in-law, put on death row, eventually in front of a firing squad (with stones, of course), and pregnant with twin boys. What kind of life could she expect to find in a world that worked against her?

Over and over again in scripture, we find individuals who the world has placed at the bottom of the totem pole of life. They are considered to be folks of little or no value. Yet, God in His infinite wisdom takes these folks and uses them in His divine plan for humanity. Tamar found herself on the list of "Who's Who" in the elite list of people who were blood-related to Jesus.

There is an old saying that goes like this, "You can't tell a book by its cover!" Unfortunately, people are so often judged by what is seen. The tendency in dealing with folks that don't match up to our standard is to isolate them by ignoring them. They are not our kind of people. I don't understand their religion. They use a different Bible. You can't trust these people. The list goes on and on, all about what is different.

The scripture says God looks beyond the outward appearance and looks upon the heart of a person. Can we do likewise? Can we get beyond the outward appearance of a person and see the real human being that is before us? Can we take into account the common ground that all earthlings share? Can we embrace what is different and appreciate it for what it is, a person seeking to live a meaningful life?

The scriptures tell us, "We often entertain angels unaware!" This scripture suggests angels often take the form of human beings in order to function as God's messengers. Some years ago, a TV program named "Touched by An Angel" used this concept.

Has your life been touched by an angel?

26

My Brother's Keeper

He didn't have to go, but he wanted to go. He did not want to remain in a safe place while most of his men were out on daily missions that brought them face-to-face with a fierce enemy in the Iraqi War. He wanted to go with them to experience the dangers they faced on a daily basis. His encouragement came from his participation and not just the handing out of orders. He led by example. Command Sergeant Major (CSM) Cook was the top enlisted non-commissioned officer in the First Brigade Germany. A lot of his work was done behind a desk while sorting through matters that called for his direct attention.

He was determined not to be a leader of just "Do what I say," but to be a leader of "Do as I do." So, on this particular day down range (Iraq), he rode along with his soldiers to the various points of contact with the enemy. While I'm not sure of all the details, somewhere along the way, the Hum-V in which he was riding passed over an Improvised Explosive Device (IED), which exploded. CSM Cook was killed instantly. In an attempt to better serve his men, CSM Cook lost his life. He knew the dangers he would face going down range, but he did it anyway. CSM Cook and the other men who died that day were a band of brothers. They were family. They were their brother's keepers.

It was Christmas Eve, and for a great number of folks, a time of celebration. But, for the Cook family, it would be a time of grief, emptiness, and anger. Someone has said "War is Hell." I can think of no better picture of hell than a battlefield where men come together to kill one another. In the true sense of the word, there are no winners in war; only survivors. War destroys our sense of humanity. So at the end of a war, there are individuals and nations that have survived. They are challenged to accept their wounds, try to heal and go on with their lives.

Easier said than done! While the soldiers coming back from war may or may not have any visible wounds on the outside, their minds and inner souls have been impacted by the negative energy of war. Many returning soldiers seek out some sort of substance to help them forget and deal with the memories that won't go away. Others continue the use of alcohol and drugs that were available in the war zone. Their substance of choice, rather than being a helping component, continues to take the soldier further and further away from the feelings and emotions they need to claim in order to recover and heal.

"Houston, we have a problem!" It seems we are better at going to war than we are at dealing with all the problems and issues wars bring back home. In 2014, communities across the country identified 49,933 homeless veterans. While we have come up with better ideas on seeking out and finding the enemy and destroying them, we have not been as good at finding our homeless veterans to bring them back into mainline society.

It was Cain who made the statement, "Am I my brother's keeper?" He said that after killing his brother. It was his response to God who had asked the question, "Where is your brother?" We seek to kill that which threatens our well-being or threatens to take from us that which we are not willing to give up. At those times, being our brother's keeper is not our top priority. No matter what transpires, the question will come back to us, "Where is your brother? Where is your sister? What have God's people done to one another?"

That question came up again one day as Jesus traveled about the countryside. A lawyer stood up and asked what he needed to do to inherit eternal life. Jesus responded with a question. "How do you interpret the Law of Moses?"

The man responded, "You should love God with all your heart, mind, soul and your neighbor as yourself."

"That's right," Jesus responded. "Now, all you have to do is follow through with that, and you shall live."

But, there was still one more question the lawyer wished to know; "Who is my neighbor?"

At that point Jesus told the story of what has become known as "The Good Samaritan." It could just as well be called "The Good Outlaw" or "The Good Muslim." In other words, you may put in the name of a group of people that you consider to be the greatest threat to your well-being. Put in the name of the person you dislike the most, a person you would not want to be caught dead with. That's the name that should go in the blank space.

The newspaper article read: ". . .a man was robbed and beaten almost to the point of death just off of Highway 74 out of Jerusalem." A local minister said he saw the man on his way to church, but was running late so he did not have time to stop and check on him. A deacon at the same church gave a similar report. The report had it that one of the homeless veterans living in the woods came out and got help for the man who was then taken to a local hospital. The ambulance driver said the homeless fellow gave him $1.37 in change to help the man. Another EMS worker said she thought this was all the money the homeless fellow had.

The follow-up question by Jesus was: "Who of these three do you think was neighbor to this man?"

The most unlikely person in the world had filled the role as neighbor to the person beaten and robbed. There was good reason for the pastor and deacon to pass by the victim. It was a dangerous thing to do to stop and render help. It might have been an attempt to lure them into a trap. It might have cost them their lives. So, with this in mind, the priest (pastor) and the Levite (deacon) decided to pass on by. The most unlikely person in the world stopped and fulfilled the role as neighbor.

Likewise, Jesus went about His business of being a good neighbor to one and all. He helped people no one else would help. He stopped and took time to give assistance to a variety of folks who were wounded in an assortment of ways and were in desperate need of help. They needed love, forgiveness, and acceptance as persons worthy of care. While a lot of us pick and choose who is worthy of our time and energy, Jesus simply took it as the opportunity presented itself. He never asked the question: "Is this worth my time and effort?" That question never came into the equation.

God gives us opportunities to fulfill our roles as good neighbors. We may ignore them, or we may embrace them. It depends on the depth of our compassion for the least among us. Compassion enables us to get out of our comfort zone and to do the right thing. It enables us to keep being the good neighbor instead of passing the role on to someone else.

In the Gospel according to Matthew, Jesus described the person who had embraced the role as neighbor. Jesus told His listeners: "I was hungry and you gave me food; I was thirsty and you gave me water to drink; I was a stranger and you gave me your best hospitality; I was naked and you gave me clothes to wear; I was sick and you took care of me; I was in jail and you came to see me."

When these people asked, "When did we do all these things for you?" Jesus responded, "When you do it unto the least of humanity, you do it to me."

Have you had any good neighbor opportunities?

27

Rough & Tumble

Miss McFarland, our third grade teacher, believed boys had too much energy, so she always set aside some time after lunch for "rough and tumble." She believed boys would be less trouble if they allowed to work off all this extra energy. The whole event was a free-for-all. The boys wrestled one another until the teacher called, "Time up."

You might think that activity rather simple to do, but it seemed I never got it right. On one occasion, someone hit me in the stomach, which knocked the breath out of me. I doubled over and fell to the floor. My teacher called me over and told me if I couldn't take it, I needed to sit with her and the girls. That was not what I wanted to do, but I had no choice in the matter. How embarrassing!

On another day during rough and tumble, I was getting some revenge on the classmate who had hit me in the stomach. My teacher must have thought I was getting too much revenge, so she called me over again and told me if I couldn't play right, I would have to stop doing rough and tumble and sit with her and the girls. So from that point on, I was not allowed to participate in rough and tumble, which led to some name-calling about sitting with the girls. It just seemed third grade was like a giant mountain that loomed over my life with my not knowing how to go over or around it.

I felt confused about the whole matter, but I was afraid to approach Miss McFarland about it. I didn't want to upset her any more, so I just kept quiet. She was an authority figure I didn't want to confront. Stuffing my feelings down inside me was my way of coping. I felt embarrassed about being put with the girls. Something must be wrong with me! At recess, some of the boys and girls in my class kept reminding me I must be a sissy. There was not much I could do about it. If I got into a

WALKING IN GRANDPA'S FOOTSTEPS: STORIES OF GOD'S GRACE AND MERCY

fight with any of the boys, it would only get me deeper in trouble with my teacher. Better leave things alone!

It got so I hated to go out for recess and endure the name-calling. It just wasn't worth it. Today, this would be called "bullying." I'd like to just forget my whole third-grade year, but like a bad habit, the thoughts keep coming back again and again. I compare it to a tattoo. Once you get it one, it's hard to get rid of it.

It's experiences like this that give self-esteem a bad name. I can't say this was the root of my poor self-image and lack of self-confidence, but it surely didn't help matters any. I have had problems with self-esteem all my life. I realize I don't stand alone with these issues. I never thought I was smart enough in school. I recently came across all my report cards from first grade through the twelfth grade, and I marvel how I made it through school. I think my average grade was somewhere between a D+ and a C-. So, the proof is in the pudding!

Those of us who struggle with negative self-esteem have a close affinity with the woman Jesus met at Jacob's well as described in the fourth chapter of the Gospel according to John. She was a Samaritan woman, which meant she came from the other side of the tracks. Samaritans were considered to be a half-breed. Apparently, she did not have a good reputation in the city of Sychar, because being at the well in the middle of the day, rather than later on in the afternoon or early evening hours showed the other women of the city had nothing to do with her.

When she came up to the well, Jesus asked her for a drink of water. She was surprised by his request, and we hear the inner voice controlling the outer voice, "How is it that you, being a Jew, ask a drink of water from me? I am a woman of Samaria."

Then the writer of the Gospel stated, "For Jews have no dealings with the Samaritans." The woman was as low as you could get on the "Totem

Pole of Life." Even her own people had nothing to do with her. She was isolated (marginalized). When the disciples returned from town, they, too, wondered why Jesus was talking with this woman. Apparently, her reputation was known far and wide. The outer voices of the other women of the village seemed to resonate with her critical inner voice. It was this critical inner voice that continued to control her life.

There is another component of the story of the woman at the well, and that is the "Jesus factor." She met someone who believed in her and saw what she could become if she put her mind to it. An encounter with that stranger made all the difference in the world to her. Many Biblical scholars believe she was Mary Magdalene, who was the last person at the cross and the first person at the tomb. She was also the first person to preach the Good News of our risen Lord. The disciples who were hidden away in the upper room were her first congregation. Imagine, a woman with such damaged self-esteem overcoming her critical inner voice and finding her true voice. She found a positive voice that allowed her to experience the liberation and freedom our Lord seeks to bestow upon all of us.

In their book, *Self-Esteem*, Matthew McKay and Patrick Fanning state self-esteem is a necessary component of life. There is a unique capacity we *homosapiens* (human beings) have over the other members of the planet, and that is the capacity to judge and evaluate the meaning and worth of our lives.

So the question becomes, in spite of what others have done to us and more important, what we have done to ourselves, "How can we find our true voice, the positive voice within us?" First of all, we need to confront our biggest critic. Our inner voice which tells us we are not good enough! We are damaged goods. That is the voice we must confront.

We need to say to the inner voice, "You're crazy, I'm a lot better than that! You don't know who I really am and what I can do if I put my mind to it." Every time a critical, negative thought comes to mind, you must challenge it. You can't let your critical voice get away with anything. When the voice rises up, put it down. Eventually, you will be able to hear the positive inner voice, which has been silenced by the critical voice. Once you start listening to your positive inner voice, your self-esteem will rise to the top. The wall around you will disappear, and you will experience a freedom of expression and integration that will bring you into new possibilities.

Which voice is controlling your life?

28

Santa Lied

The little girl was all excited! The day had come for her first visit with Santa Claus. Although she was only three at the time, she had some awareness of the importance of this trip. Her one desire for Christmas was a push scooter, and she wasted no time telling that to Santa. So, Taylor Loran Mosser departed from her visit with Santa with high expectations. All she had to do now was to wait for Christmas morning to come, and her dreams would come true.

On Christmas morning, she was up early and made sure her parents were up as well. In no time at all, wrapping paper was flying in all directions as each present was unwrapped. When all the presents had been exposed, there was no push scooter to be found. Hey, something had gone wrong here! "Where's my scooter?" she asked. Lauran and Jason assured Taylor Santa had passed the task over to her great-grandfather. To this diplomatic attempt, Taylor responded, "Santa li-ded!" Her parents tried to assure her Santa had not lied to her, but their efforts were in vain.

Children teach us how to be excited about unknown gifts and how to dream of what could possibly come true. We should not stop being excited about the gifts God offers. We should not stop dreaming of what could be and what God would like to see happen in our lives. Our journey through life should contain a vision of what we can do and what we can become.

In the Book of Joel, found in the Old Testament, we are told: "It shall come to pass afterward that I will pour out My Spirit on all flesh; your sons and your daughters shall have thoughts of their future, your men and women shall dream dreams, your young men and women shall see visions." Joel 2: 28 (Paraphrase by RLF)

Some of my hopes and dreams have come true and some have not, but I have been so blessed with those that have that I have no regrets. Some of the most valuable gifts I have received in my life were a total surprise to me. I have asked God for a lot of things, but it has been the things I didn't ask for that have made the biggest difference in my life.

I have this belief that God gives us the gift we need rather than the gift we want. In order for us to receive what God has given through the Christ child, we need to be willing to unravel all the wrappings around our lives that prevent us from discovering the deeper meaning of God's gift to us.

We may say Santa represents a spirit of wonder and excitement of the unopened gift. It still remains, the manger scene begs the question, "Who is this child, and what does this gift mean for my life?"

Is there a gift you have left unwrapped?

29

Searching for Snakes

The road was like some obstacle course! At times, I believed the entire Jeep would disappear in a rut. Fortunately for me, the Jeep had four-wheel drive (4WD) and was able to handle the deep crevices in the road. If your body was still in one piece after the 20-mile trip to the top of Hogback Mountain, then you were one of the fortunate few.

This was my weekly trip up the 3,211-foot slope, which was the location of the transmitter site for WSPA-TV/FM in Spartanburg, South Carolina. I worked there as an engineer, maintaining the TV and FM radio transmitters. On this occasion I had company, which included five members of my youth group from Grace Baptist Church. As the youth director, I planned weekly activities for the youth and tried to enhance their understanding of God. So Junior Smith, Terry Shields, Johnny Kimbrall, Randy McHenry, and Jerry Smith were my companions that day. I had informed them there was not a lot to do up there, but they could explore the remains of an abandoned golf course and clubhouse built back in the 1920s. That was okay with them, but what they really wanted to do was search for snakes.

So away we went to the top of the mountain! Hogback Mountain had been a booming place in the early years of the 20th century until the stock market crash in 1929. After that, it all dried up, then the weeds and bushes took over. I understood some of the clubhouse and the Olympic-size swimming pool were still visible. If the boys wanted snakes, that would be a good place to find them.

Upon arrival, I had a briefing from the engineer going off duty. After the briefing, he took the Jeep back down the mountain. A normal tour of duty was 24 hours, but there have been times when snow and sleet had prevented anyone from coming up or down the mountain. On those occasions I had been up there alone for three or four days. There was always plenty of food in the freezer and refrigerator so on those occasions you wouldn't starve. Clyde Burdette, our chief engineer, made sure our supplies were maintained.

I showed the boys the various transmitters, and gave them a brief overview of the process we used to receive a signal from the Spartanburg studio and then broadcast it to the surrounding areas. Yes, that was a time before cable TV, when you got your TV shows by an antenna on top of your house. The second floor of the building contained the transmitters, while the first floor housed our generator, which came into play if the power went out. Also on the second floor was a large patio that allowed you to look out over the landscape below. On nights when the sky was clear, you could Spartanburg in the distance.

The boys decided to wait until the next morning before making their Lewis and Clark expedition. Their plans included catching some rattlesnakes or anything else that might be available to them. I warned them that if they were bitten, the trip to the hospital would not be a quick one. So be careful! I didn't tell them the only kind of snakes I'm afraid of are the live ones and the dead ones.

Come Saturday morning, they were off on their excursion. Around lunchtime they returned with several snakes that had had the misfortune of crossing their path. Among the snakes was a rattlesnake, which was their pride and joy. I suppose it was their way of living on the edge of life and death and the rush of adrenaline that made their adventure worthwhile.

It was a dangerous thing to do, but they all made it through the experience. After a short break for lunch, they were off again for more adventure. I went out on the patio to look for them and found them climbing up the TV tower, which was 275 feet high. I called them back, because the exposure from the FM and TV antennas can cause some serious health problems. Being on the tower was only allowed when both transmitters were turned off around 1:00 AM.

Later that afternoon, my replacement arrived, and soon the boys and I were on our way back to civilization. As we made our descent down the mountain, I thanked God everyone was safe and sound. The building at the top was still standing, and no one had been bitten by a snake. I think they may have brought back a few chigger bites they picked up from the blueberry bushes that grew near our TV site.

Recently, I got together with my former youth group for the first time in 40 years. It was a delightful evening of fellowship, food and laughter. In spite of all the years that had gone by, we rediscovered our love and compassion for one another. Yes, we had been separated for many years, but the bond was still intact. It was a great time for me to be together with folks I had journeyed with in my early years of ministry. It was a time of spiritual renewal for me, as I once again was reminded of my call to a Christian vocation and the youth group that had provided so much encouragement for me. Just being in their presence was all I needed. It brought healing to my mind, body, and spirit. Surely God was in our midst, and we knew it not. His Spirit blew across our lives that night. That is the source of our unity. That is how we and the rest of the world are held together. It does not come about by what we do, but what we don't do. The Psalmist reminded us that in our stillness the creative work of God is more powerful than any other time in our lives. It is in our silence that the voice of God speaks the loudest through our lives.

That night, we created fellowship, which said to one and all: "We belong to God, we belong to one another, and we belong to the world and beyond." In that small room at the Clock Drive-In was a microcosm of the life God called all of us to embrace. As we embrace one another, we embrace God.

Searching for snakes! To a lot of people, the snake is hated and despised just for being a snake. Unfortunately, this attitude prevails in our world filled with different people and different cultures. They are often treated like snakes. They are disliked just for being who they are and not for any particular thing they have done. They are to be avoided, and some folks even think to be killed.

In John's vision found in the Book of Revelation, he said he saw a new heaven and a new earth coming down from God. While some folks see this as dropping out of the sky, this vision does not preclude a renewal of the old heaven and earth. In fact, it could very well point to the historical event of the birth of Jesus. He brings a new dimension of God from heaven and a new creation to earth. The new heaven and earth God envisioned for us becomes a reality in this person. If His words and actions are taken to heart, we will truly live as a civilized people, accepting one another as members of God's family. Instead of trying to destroy one another because of various differences, we will embrace the whole person who stands before us.

The question that confronts us is, "Can we allow this new creation to begin in us?"

30

She Had a Dream

She was a young lady in her late teens and staying with some relatives in Columbia, South Carolina. She and her sister had come to the big city from the small rural community in Polk County, North Carolina. They were seeking to see what else the world had to offer and enjoying some freedom away from home.

One of the relatives was the CEO of a hospital in Columbia, so it was at that time Emma Lou Skipper discovered the vocation of nursing. While growing up on the farm back home, she had had a lot of experience taking care of her younger brothers and sisters. So, the opportunity to go into a vocation that seemed suited for her was an exciting thought.

In a correspondence with her mother back home, Emma Lou revealed her desire to go into nursing. The return correspondence from her mother was a flat "No." No, nursing was not a proper vocation to pursue in the late 1930s and early1940s. So with that response, Emma Lou laid aside her plans.

The expectation was she would get married and raise a family like all the other young ladies. So, she did just that! Ralph Ford was a handsome young man from the big town of Ruth, North Carolina, to whom she was introduced to by her sister, Adlena. Their courtship was rather short, and soon they were off to Gaffney, South Carolina, to get married. A year later, they had a son who was named after his two great-grandparents, Robert Ford and Loran Wilson. Loran Wilson was born on December 19, 1868, and young Robert was born on December 19, 1944. So Emma Lou put her life into raising her son, "Bob," as he would be called.

At the age of 14, Bob was at the local skating rink when he fell and broke his left arm. It was a compound fracture. The first surgery did not go so well. The doctors informed his parents the arm would be crooked. Well, this was not going to happen to the Fords' only son, so a group of specialists was contacted and a second surgery performed with success. The only problem: the insurance company would only pay for the first surgery, not the second.

Emma Lou set out to find a job that would help pay for this surgery. She took a job at Spartanburg General Hospital as a nurse's aide. Later on, she was given the opportunity of going to nursing school to become a Licensed Practical Nurse (LPN). After several years of school, she finally reached her lifetime goal when she took on the new role of being an LPN.

What had started out as a bad experience at the skating rink had led to Emma Lou's lifetime dream coming true. Out of a bad situation, God had brought forth an opportunity of a lifetime for Emma Lou. She had entered the nursing program offered at Spartanburg General Hospital and two years later, she had her nursing degree.

Proverbs 29: 18 says that "Without a vision, the people perish!"

Then we have these words from the Prophet Joel: "It shall come to pass that I will pour out my spirit upon all flesh; sons and daughters shall have a vision of the future; adults shall have dreams; I hold nothing back, I empty out my spirit upon all humanity." Joel 2: 28-29 (Paraphrase by RLF)

The dreams go both ways! They are not only about our vision of what we would like to do with our lives, but also God's vision for us of what He can accomplish in our lives.

Sweet dreams!

31

She's Still My Friend

The voice from the back seat kept repeating, "How much longer will it be?"

Over and over again those words rang out from the back seat, and over and over again the answer from the front seat would be, "Not as long as it was." We were on our way to Myrtle Beach, South Carolina, with our granddaughter, Taylor Loran Mosser. The trip that originated in Hickory, North Carolina, would take about four hours. I'm not sure if we had gotten much farther than the city limits when this question was first sounded.

We finally made our way to the hotel resort, and soon our granddaughter was out in the pool. Gail, my wife, took her place under a big umbrella with a favorite book, and I played water games with Taylor. Eventually, Taylor made some friends, so at that time I went back to the big umbrella for a much-needed break.

On one occasion, Gail took a break and went back to our room, while I stayed at the pool with our granddaughter. She was playing with another little girl, and as they were jumping around and playing the little girl went underwater and got strangled. She then went crying to her mother, saying our granddaughter had pushed her under the water.

At the same time, Taylor came running to me, pleading her case. Taylor was younger, but a more experienced swimmer than her playmate. I informed Taylor that what she had done had scared the little girl. Taylor's response was from the mouths of babes: "I'm still her friend," she said, with tears in her eyes.

"Yes," I said, "I know you are, but you need to apologize to her for what you did." With that bit of encouragement, Taylor went over to the little girl and her mother and apologized. Soon Taylor and the little girl were back in the water playing again.

As I sat there under the big umbrella, I thought of how much better off our world would be if we adults could say we are sorry when our actions have caused hurt and pain to another person. In the TV series, "Happy Days," the Fonz could never say he was sorry. That word was just not in his vocabulary. While he may have had problems, it is a word we should become very comfortable using.

Scripture tells us not to "allow the sun to go down on our anger." In other words, don't hoard up the negative stuff that life brings to our door. The quicker we get rid of it, the better off we will be. Holding on to grudges and ill feelings toward others who have hurt us will do us no good in the long run.

We need to choose carefully what parts of our past we want to carry around with us. Some things we need to hold on to and other things we need to let go of. By this, we may find peace with ourselves, our families, our community, and our God.

While my granddaughter's actions were unintentional, a lot of hurt and pain in our world has an intentional component about it. That is not easily fixed. It generally takes more than an "I'm sorry." Sometimes a professional counselor is needed to help sort through the bad stuff and to bring some redemption and understanding to the situation.

It only takes one person to cause a break in a relationship, but it takes a minimum of two to put it back together again. Again from the cross, we have the words of Jesus: "Forgive them Father, for they know not what they have done."

Is there someone in your life you need to ask for forgiveness? Is there someone you need to forgive?

32

Stranded

I knew the old car was on its last leg, but I was still driving it back and forth from work and on my weekend trips with the Army Reserve, which at times took me all over both North and South Carolina. The 1978 Chevrolet Monza had over 260,000 miles under its belts, but it was still getting the job done. As I was coming home one Sunday afternoon from Spartanburg, South Carolina, the old car just "laid down and died" on me. It was a quick death, and I don't believe it suffered very much in the process. Knowing the end was near, I pulled over to the side of the road where my car took its last breath. It was a sad ending for an old friend.

So there I was just outside of Spartanburg on I-85 Business—stranded. Lucky for me, it was a nice day—a mild day, in fact, for early October 1986. Those were the days before cell-phones, so it was necessary for me to walk to the nearest gas station to call for help. On my way there, I looked back at my car and noticed another car had pulled in front of it. So, I made my way back to see who had stopped.

It was a family from Pickens, South Carolina, who were on their way to Charlotte, North Carolina, to see some family members. They had seen me walking down the interstate with my Army fatigues on and my car parked on the side of the road. Upon reaching their car, I explained to them that my car had quit running and I was in the process of getting to a phone to call my wife in Vale, North Carolina, to come and get me.

"No, need," they said. "We just recently bought this car, and we are on our way to Charlotte to visit with some of our relatives, but we have time to take you in the direction of home."

I told them Vale was quite a distance out of their way, but if they would drop me off at the Shelby exit, I could get my wife to pick me up there. "No, that won't be necessary, we can take you home. It won't be any trouble at all. Besides, we haven't been up that way in a long time. It'll be a good trip for us." Everyone in the car agreed, so off we went!

On the way home, I talked about a stray Saint Bernard dog we had rescued. My wife had seen the dog outside a restaurant on our way home from Hickory. At the time, the dog was just skin and bones. We picked the dog up at the restaurant with the blessings of the restaurant owners. My wife had provided him with plenty of food, washed and groomed him, so he was back on his way to good health. I explained we did not have a good place to keep him, so we were looking for someone with a better place. The gentleman driving the car said to his wife, "I think we could use another dog down on the farm." The rest of the family agreed, so when they left my home, there was a Saint Bernard in their backseat.

Was it just luck this family from Pickens, South Carolina, came by at the time they did? How many cars traveling to and fro down I-85 Business would have stopped to help me? If there were a few cars that would stop, how many would have been willing to take me all the way to my home in Vale, North Carolina? I think maybe there was some divine intervention going on. I would have to say along with Jacob, "God was in this place and I knew it not."

Recently in Catawba County, North Carolina, a motorist stopped to help another motorist who had run off the road. When the motorist approached the car, the man inside the wrecked car pulled out a gun and shot the man who was trying to help him. The motorist died trying to do a good deed.

So, there are risks involved in helping people. That is probably the main reason the priest and the Levite in the story of the "Good Samaritan" passed the man by who had been beaten and robbed. That scenario of the "Good Samaritan's" becoming the victim has been played out many times. There is a saying: "No good deed goes unpunished."

Jesus was straight up with his audience and warned them that following him may have negative consequences. On a number of occasions he said to them, "Take up your cross and follow me." The symbol of the cross has many meanings. One of those meanings is that of suffering and death. That's the one we don't like to think about too much. Perhaps, we could say there are two sides of the cross. One side represents life and the other death.

Also, Jesus told his audience that to follow Him they must be willing to give their lives away, which in many ways might be a very painful process. Jesus warned them that by keeping their lives, they would eventually lose them and if they were willing to give their lives away, they would find them.

Jesus made it perfectly clear that to follow Him meant that we do all the good we can for everyone we can. It meant becoming involved in the lives of those who could use our help. There is nothing we can substitute for this kind of personal involvement with those who suffer in a variety of ways. I tell you, being stranded has its own kind of pain and suffering.

I am a member of a local group called "Veterans Helping Veterans." We try to help stranded veterans who live out in the woods all around the community of Hickory, North Carolina. Our vision statement is to empower veterans and their families to become secure and independent with dignity. Our mission statement is to connect veterans and their families to a network of vital community resources. We try to find homes for veterans and get them in school, help them find jobs, and provide clothes to go to a job interview. We help them with what they need to say and not say at a job interview. Our organization, along with many more in our community, tries to bring assistance to individuals and families who are stranded; that is, they have been marginalized or as Rod Serling would put it, they have been placed in the "Outer Limits" of our world.

"I was stranded, and you took the time to help me, and that has made all the difference in the world to me."

Our world is constantly changing. People are coming from all over the world to what they believe to be the promised land. If they don't have a right to be here, then neither do we! We may despise them, or we may choose to be their friend. They are the strangers in our midst. Remember the words from Matthew's Gospel: "I was a stranger, I was marginalized, I was allowed only on the peripheral edges of your community, but you still took me in. In spite of the opposition of bringing me into your world, you were willing to be a friend to me. You were willing to treat me like a human being with value. What you have done for me has made all the difference in the world to me. I will never be the same. Through you, God has drawn near to me." (Paraphrase by RLF)

Any stranded people in your world?

33

Summer Games

Ah, the last day of school and a whole summer before me to play baseball and other games with my friends in Grace Cotton Mill Village, which was nestled between the two communities of Ruth and Rutherfordton, North Carolina. On occasion, I played baseball with my cousins, Dean and Michael. They lived near the local grammar school in Ruth, which had a large playground. One of us took a turn at bat, and another pitched while the third was in the outfield. It was fairly easy to get Dean to play, but Michael always wanted to negotiate a deal in which he batted first. Since we couldn't play without him, we had to cater to his demands. Rather than go through this hassle every time, we told Michael he was batting first. Truthfully, I don't think it mattered that much to any of us who batted first. It was more important that we were all in the game and we all got our time at bat. Although we did not have a full team on the field, we enjoyed our style of baseball and we enjoyed the company of one another.

Jesus had a team that followed Him around from town to town. In all, He had 12 players who had joined with him to change the world. I think the general belief among His team was that this kingdom about which He spoke was to be set up here on earth. They imagined His kingdom would look something like the nation under King David or fairly close to it. So it was not surprising that from time to time they wondered how they would fit into this kingdom structure.

In fact, one day as Jesus and His team traveled up to Jericho, James and John pulled Jesus aside to ask a favor. The favor was to be the first of the disciples to sit one on His right and one on His left in the new kingdom. Jesus responded they did not realize what they were asking of Him. He explained the seats of honor they were asking for were not His to give away. He also explained to them what it meant to be first in His kingdom. The positions James and John were asking for had been given to two thieves on a Friday afternoon; one on His left and one on His right. Did they truly want those positions? Maybe, this picture gives a better understanding of Jesus' call to those that would follow Him to "take up their cross."

I think what James and John had in mind was their status in the Kingdom of God. It suggests their view of the Kingdom of God was from the perspective of what they could gain for their lives. On the other hand, Jesus' view of the Kingdom of God was from the perspective of self-sacrifice. The Kingdom Jesus spoke of was about how to give your life away to the purpose and will of God.

Another game that I played with my cousins was called "King of the Hill." Someone went first at being on top of a hill. The road that ran beside our grandparents' home was elevated enough to provide an incline on either side. We chose the bank that consisted of good ole Southern red clay! The rest of us tried to pull whoever was at the top off and take his place at the top. It was a child's game that imitated a component of the adult world. That is, you need to get to the top of whatever endeavor you are involved in as fast as you can and stay there as long as you can. Often, the end justifies the means! The measure of success in our world is determined by power, influence, and money. It certainly seems a lot of folks have bought into that view of life.

Jesus reminded His followers that His kingdom would not be setup that way: "To whom much is given, much will be required. To whom much is committed, much more will be asked of that person." Luke 12: 48b (Paraphrase by RLF). The Apostle Paul often spoke of being a servant of Christ. Such is the makeup of the Kingdom of God! To be a servant of Christ is to be a servant to His people. To accomplish that, we must be willing to enter into His world of self-sacrifice, which consists of robbers and thieves.

So! Do you really want to bat first? Do really want to be king of the hill?

Where do you fit in?

34

Swim or Drown

It was the day I been waiting for all week! It was Sunday, the day each summer that my family went to the river near Lake Lure. It was the summer my parents connected up with their best friends, Paul and Thelma Ford each Sunday. My goal for the summer was to learn how to swim. So my dad was determined to teach me how by using his technique of "swim or drown." Dad picked me up, and just threw me into the river believing I would figure it out and swim back to shore. It didn't work for me. I went straight to the bottom of the river and just sat there for a while until my dad reached down and pulled me to the top.

Paul had a different technique! He held me up in the water and then he told me to kick my feet and move my arms as fast as I could. Week after week we went through that same routine, with the same results, me on the bottom of the river bed. Again, my dad picked me up and just threw me into the deep water believing I needed a second chance at Plan A. It didn't happen. They had to pull me up from the bottom of the river again. So after doing this a few times, we went back to Plan B.

Again, Paul continued to encourage me to kick my feet and move my arms. I continued to attempt to get the hang of it, but it just seemed to everyone that I would be a rock in water. Paul never gave up and neither did I. Kicking my feet and moving my arms as fast as I could, I finally turned to Paul to say I was through for the day, but he wasn't there. Hey, what's going on here, I thought. I then discovered I had been swimming on my own. Paul was not holding me up, I was swimming.

I spent the rest of the afternoon perfecting my new found skill. I wondered why it took me so long to learn to do this. Well, whatever the reason, I had overcome my body's tendency to sink to the bottom of the river. I knew how to swim on my own. No one was holding me up, and no one was looking for me at the bottom of the river. That new found sense of freedom felt great. I could dive into the water and explore the bottom, knowing I could get to the top and swim back to shore.

To learn to swim, you must get into the water. You will get wet! It will spoil your hair-do! The water will probably be cold. Some just dive-in and get wet all at once, while others like myself prefer to take it slow and easy. There's nothing wrong with either approach, just one takes a little more time, but in the end the whole body gets wet.

God called all of us to immerse ourselves in a special way of life. The historical Jesus is our model! "This is how you ought to live," he says to us. This is how you ought to treat people in our world. It doesn't matter about the differences in social, cultural, political, or religious styles. The most important thing is to love all of God's people! Love your enemies! Have compassion for all people.

In the movie, *"Oh Brother, Where Art Thou,"* the trio found themselves at a river where a baptismal service was being held. One of the brothers decided to go over and find out what it's all about. It didn't take long before the preacher was baptizing him. He came back to his companions and invited them, as he put it:

"Come on in boys, the water's fine!"

The Gospel according to Matthew is the only synoptic gospel (Matthew, Mark, and Luke) to have the story of the baptism of Jesus. Jesus was baptized by John the Baptizer, as he was known by the Christian community. That event in the life of the historical Jesus represented a new direction his life would take from that point on. He would no longer work as a carpenter's apprentice, but he would now give himself to the work of the Kingdom of God.

As the baptism of Jesus was a time of receiving his vocational calling and the blessing of his Heavenly Father, so it is with all who would be his followers. Therefore, it is more than some would suppose to be only a symbolic act; it is an act of receiving the blessings and the commission of our Heavenly Father. While baptism is not a requirement for salvation, just think of it, no one took the thief next to Jesus on the cross down to be baptized, yet Jesus promised him he would be with him in paradise. Therefore, baptism is an act of receiving the blessings of God and God's commission for us.

I leave you with those famous words, "Come on in whoever you are, the water's fine." He who calls is waiting.

Are you willing to accept your calling from God?

35

Telling It like It Is

It was a cloudy, dreary morning as I looked out the window of the plane making its way to Mendenhall Air Force Base, England. This was my first trip overseas, and my mind was filled with questions about the challenges ahead.

It had been only three months into my tour of duty at Charleston Air Force Base (AFB) in South Carolina, when I received orders for Alconbury AFB in England. The general thought is, the worst AFB in the world is the one you are leaving and the best is the one you are going to. I was leaving a MAC Base (Military Airlift Command) and would soon find myself in front of the most powerful fighter jets in the world.

Upon arrival, there was in-processing to go through, which assigned barracks, provided clothing and other information concerning the base. At the time, there was an alert going on that limited what I could do and where I could go. It took me several weeks to complete the process. I soon found out that on a Tactual Air Command (TAC) Base, alerts were a common occurrence.

In addition to the official orientation the Air Force provided, there was an orientation provided by the other single soldiers in my barracks. I learned that in addition to the Airmen's Club on post the Royal Air Force (RAF) Base had several clubs for enlisted soldiers as well. One of the soldiers in my shop (work area) was going to the RAF Base and asked me to go along with him. It soon became a weekly event. Airman Skuherski drove a Volkswagen that was good transportation for the trip of about 40 miles there and back.

Eventually, we were going to some club about every night of the week. Week after week and month after month of getting into bed late and getting up at 4:00 or 5:00 AM was getting to me. A daily visitor to the Airmen's Club was Airman Ginny, as she was called, who was British. On one occasion, she made a comment about the black rings under my eyes. "Black rings? Are you kidding me?" I responded. I immediately went back to the barracks and took a good look at myself in the mirror. Sure enough, there they were—three or four black-looking rings under both eyes.

I decided then and there, I had to make some changes in my life, so I told Airman Skuherski I wouldn't be going on our weekly trips. Well, it took more than one person dropping out for Skuherski to stop his routine. He went over to the RAF Base that night by himself, and on the way back hit a bad place in the road and ended up hitting a tree spot-on. Skuherski was banged up a bit, but not hurt seriously. The authorities who investigated the wreck said if someone had been riding in the passenger seat, they would have been killed instantly.

Well, apparently God was not through with me. If it had not been for Airman Ginny's making the comments she did, I would have been in that seat. Man, what a close call! Airman Ginny and I crossed paths just at the right time. Although she had a rather quiet demeanor, for some reason she decided to confront me about how I looked. It got my attention!

At times, we need to cross paths with someone who will tell us like it is. We need to hear the truth about ourselves, and we need to hear it straight on. We often deceive ourselves into believing we are okay when we are not. We need to be open to the truth about ourselves no matter the source from which it comes to us.

The prophets of Israel, in spite of the risks, told it like it was and pointed out what the people needed to do to correct their condition. Generally speaking, we don't like someone telling us what changes we need to make in our lives. Of course, there needs to be some diplomacy in how such news is delivered. Having a sense of the right time and place is of importance, but sometimes some things just need to be said to someone going in the wrong direction.

While we normally think of preachers as being the source of such news, the scriptures bear witness that God uses a variety of people and sometimes animals to deliver His message. Unfortunately, the general rule is to kill the messenger. This procedure is called "scapegoating." The term is taken from the practice of the high priest to "lay the sins" of his people on a goat and then send it out into the desert as a symbolic gesture of God's taking the sins away from His people. Therefore, when we ascribe our bad behavior to someone else rather than taking personal responsibility for our actions, we are guilty of scapegoating.

The "Flip Wilson Philosophy" of the devil made me do it won't work here. As the song goes, it's not my brother or sister, but it's me, Lord, standing in the need of prayer. If we have one or two people in our lives who will tell us like it is, then we have been greatly blessed of God.

Jesus instructs his followers as recorded in the Gospel of John that "the truth will set them free" if they continue to abide in His word. His word may come to us like a deck of cards, in the form of a diamond (a reward) or of a heart (compassion) or a club (discipline) or a spade (a challenge). Whatever form the truth takes in our lives, it comes not to destroy us but to bring healing and wholeness. This is always God's goal of telling us like it is!

Can you handle God's truth for your life?

36

The Big Explosion

It was a typical gas station for the 1950s. The motto was "Happy Motoring," which meant someone from the station would come out to your car and ask you how much gas you wanted and then put the gas in your tank. While the gas was being pumped, someone from the station would clean your windshield and check the oil. Rain or shine, you got fast, convenient service from your friendly gas station attendants.

In the small community of Forest City, North Carolina, a gas station had become available, so my Uncle George decided to have a go at the business. In addition to gasoline and oil, my uncle also provided a repair service. That meant the station would have either a hydraulic lift or a grease pit for a car to be driven over, and the mechanic could then go down the steps into the grease pit to work.

My uncle had enlisted the help of one of his sons, Harold, and one of Harold's good friends. It seemed that one day, while the grease pits were not in use, Harold and his friend discovered a large amount of gasoline in one of the pits. They wondered what would happen if they dropped a match into the gasoline. So, one of them went down into the pit and waited for the other one to light a match and hand it to him.

The match was lit and the transfer was about to take place; when the match burned the waiting fingers of the person in the pit. Like the baton of a relay race when a runner misses the handle and allows it to fall to the ground so did the match that day. There was a loud explosion and when the smoke cleared, two young men lay out in the street. How they lived through this, I do not know. My cousin, Harold, spent a week or more in the local hospital with burns over most of his body. I can't recall how my cousin's friend fared in all of that, but he did make it through the ordeal. Both young men were fortunate to be alive.

WALKING IN GRANDPA'S FOOTSTEPS: STORIES OF GOD'S GRACE AND MERCY

Sometimes, we may risk our lives in a foolish act, not knowing what we are getting into. Like my cousin and his friend! They failed to see the risks involved in their actions. Be advised, they never tried that trick again. They had learned from their mistake. Unfortunately, many folks never seem to learn from their life experiences. There is a bit of wisdom in the expression about those who refuse to learn from their mistakes being doomed to repeat them.

Just think about it: a little girl in Kansas made the mistake of wondering away from home and was blown away by a huge storm to a faraway land. It was a time of great struggle and fear, uncertainty, and doubt. But when she returned home, she was a different person. The storm that burst into her life made all the difference in the world. Looking back on her experience, she would not change anything.

There was once a man who was angry with some people who threatened his way of life. In his eyes, they were very dangerous people and a great threat to all the people in his land. It seemed they were getting stronger and stronger in their ability to get many of his people to follow them. There was a simple solution to that sort of threat! All he needed to do was to come up with a plan to destroy them. Wipe them off the face of the earth and be done with them.

He was in the capital city one day, and as fate would have it, he was presented with an opportunity to put his plan to work. That day many of those dangerous heretics were being execution. Their death did not trouble him, because they were going to hell anyway. In a way he liked the results, so he decided to go to another large city about 100 miles north of his location. In those acts, he declared himself to be judge, jury, and executioner.

So off he went with his entourage to protect God from this onslaught of worthless and godless hoard of demon-possessed men, women, and children. His God would be proud of him for eliminating that threat from the land. He felt a little like the historical figure that killed a giant of a man who threatened God's holy and special people. Well, that wasn't going to happen under his watch.

As often happens to our best-laid plans, something gets in our way. He was about halfway to this large metropolitan city when he ran across an improvised explosive device (IED). There was a loud explosion and a voice from the explosion spoke directly to him. "What are you doing to my people? Why are you killing the people I have called to do my work in the world?" The man could not answer! He was blind, mute, and deaf.

Several days later, the man and his entourage reached the city, where they met some of the people they had intended to destroy. That was an odd turn of events! Surprisingly, the people there knew of him and the executions that had taken place in the capital city. Was this a crazy world or what? The people he had come to kill were attending to his wounds. But, the most surprising thing that happened to him was when one of the men stepped forward and touched his blind eyes. He could now see! He had a change of heart! The enemy was now a friend! It changed his destiny!

The explosion, which at first he thought was the worst thing ever to happen to him, he now saw through his spiritual eyes. God was in the explosion and he knew it not. From the explosion came a new destiny for his life. From that point on, he followed the One whose light had shown upon him. In time, he advanced the cause of the One he called Lord to the far reaches of the known world.

He discovered his ability to write inspiring letters to others who were seeking to follow his Lord. Out of his former religious faith, he developed an extensive theology that would change the world. Eventually, he found himself on the other side of the fence. The people he once represented were now out to kill him and in time they did just that.

Sometimes our best-laid plans and our deepest dreams just disintegrate before our eyes, and we discover all the king's horses and all the king's men cannot put us back together again. That unfortunate event is sometimes described as "It just blew up in my face!" or "Things just fell apart!" For some of us, it takes an earth-shattering event to get our attention. For others, it may just require a simple tap on the shoulder.

Into which category do you fall?

37

The Breezeway

It was the year my parents decided to take a vacation in Charleston, South Carolina. As we drove through the beautiful southern city, we came upon the shoreline. Some of the most beautiful homes of the city can be seen along this shoreline which has become known as "The Battery." The name was taken from a Civil War Artillery Battery that was positioned there.

To endure the high humidity, each house was built with a hallway down the center of the house on each level. Screen doors and windows allowed the wind from the bay to come rushing into the house. The breeze that made its way through the house was a welcome guest. It was like stepping out on your porch in the early morning hours and breathing in the fresh air from the ocean. Good stuff in, bad stuff out!

Without the breezeway, life in the homes would have become almost unbearable. The stale air along with the high humidity had a way of causing meltdowns among the families who lived there. These homes were built way before the modern convenience of air conditioning came along, so a breezeway was the best solution to the everyday problem of hot, stale air.

In a similar fashion, how we construct our lives determines our ability to allow the bad stuff we experience to circulate in and out. Some lives are like a sponge: they seem to absorb all the bad stuff and hold on to it like it was gold. When we collect all the bad stuff that comes our way and never let go of it, we end up with a negative view of life. Somebody is always trying to do us in. Rather than see the possibilities in others, we focus on the negative. Unfortunately, all the bad stuff that has accumulated also obscures our view of self. From time to time, we need to take an inventory of what we need to keep and what we need to allow to pass on through. We need to process our hurts and pains in order to heal.

Why hold onto hurtful things that we have experienced as a child or an adult? Like the families of the Hatfields and the McCoys after the Civil War, the hatred and desire for revenge destroyed both families. Sometimes the best we can say is "Father, forgive them, for they know not what they have done to me." It might also be appropriate to say, "Forgive me, Father, for what I have done to hurt someone else."

If we wait around for an apology, we may never get one. We need to forgive without being asked for forgiveness the same way God does us. Of course, it is better when the persons who have hurt us come to us and seek to make amends, but that does not always happen enough in our world. Bitterness makes a poor companion. We need to let go of it.

The Gospel according to Luke 19: 1 – 10, tells the story of Zacchaeus the tax collector. He's the guy who climbed up into the tree so he could get a better view of Jesus as He came passing through. To his surprise, Jesus invited Zack to have dinner with him. That was a surprise to the other folks there as well, because they did not like this man who had cheated them out of money for so many years. After having lunch with Jesus, Zack changed his ways and paid back all the money he had stolen—not just what he owed them, but ten times what he owed.

Even though Zack did his part in making things right with the people he had cheated, there were still a number of folks who would not let go of the hatred they felt toward him. They chose to keep the bad stuff. Like the song by Kenny Rodgers, "The Gambler," you need to know which cards to hold onto and which cards to throw away.

The secret to a happy and contented life is to feel the breeze! Absorb the good! Let go of the bad!

Can you do this?

38

The Bunkmate from Hell

The road from Spartanburg, South Carolina, to Charlotte, North Carolina, was a long and winding road in the summer of 1965. I had been there and back a couple of times already without much success. Family and friends gathered at the bus station several times to send me off on my tour of duty with the Air Force only to have me return the next day. Maybe, the third time was charm! I could still hear their shouts as the bus drove away, "Hey, Ford, see you tomorrow."

Three weeks before, I had stood looking at a sign with a finger pointing out at me. The message was simple, "Uncle Sam Wants You." My deferment was up, now that I had spent two years at Spartanburg Technical College in the electronic technology course. With an Associate in Science Degree in hand, I was now ready to go out and set the world on fire, but Uncle Sam wanted the first shot at me. With the Vietnam War going on, I knew my number would be coming up soon in the ongoing draft. A number of my friends had joined the Air Force, so I decided that was what I wanted to do.

So this was my third trip to the big city, because on the first two occasions their quota had been met for the week by the time I arrived. The day was September 14, 1965. Mary Sue, my mother's sister. would pick me up at the bus station. After I spent the night with her family, she would drop me off at the military processing center the next morning. I made it into the group that would go through the various medical exams to determine physical eligibility. It was a grueling day of exams from head to toe, and at the end of the day each person would be called to the front desk to find out if he or she had made it or not. My name was finally called out around 2:00 PM, so I went forward to find out my fate.

WALKING IN GRANDPA'S FOOTSTEPS: STORIES OF GOD'S GRACE AND MERCY

The officer who had more stripes on his uniform than I had years of life was slowly looking over my paperwork. I stood there in silence waiting for his word of approval or rejection. It is times like this that life seems to just trickle by at a slow pace. Finally, he looked up at me and said, "Mr. Robert Loran Ford, welcome to the United States Air Force. You will take the oath of office at 3:30 in the conference room to my left. Be reminded, as long as you are in the room when the oath is read, whether you actually say the words or not, you are considered to be sworn in as a member of the United States Air Force."

At 3:30 PM I was sworn in and at 5:00 PM I was on a plane bound for San Antonio, Texas and Lackland Air Force Base. We arrived at the airport in San Antonio at 11:00 PM, and as we casually walked into the airport terminal the air police met us. We were ordered to stand with our hands up against the wall as we were searched from head to toe for weapons of any kind. A military bus took us from the airport to the base, and after being assigned a barracks and a bunk, we finally got to bed around 2:30 AM. Wake up that morning was at 5:00 AM, which came very early that day. I ended up on the upper bunk and my bunkmate on the lower.

Bunkmates had to work together in order to make it through basic training. If one of us was at a formation and the other was not, it went down that we both were absent. Not good! It seems I had the honor of having William Hadley Jones, III, as my bunkmate. Jones was from the state of Massachusetts, and his family was high on the socioeconomic scale in Boston. Mr. Jones, now Airman Jones, was accustomed to getting things his way, so his dominating personality blew me away. Here extrovert meets introvert, and the latter is not fairing too well. Beyond getting his way all the time, the thing that bothered me the most was how he spoke to me. It went from "You dumb ass SOB" to "You ignorant bastard!" My life experience had been that fighting back always got me in trouble. Being new to the Air Force, I didn't want to do anything that would start me off in a negative direction. So for the most part, I just took his barrage of name-calling each morning and evening.

On one particular evening after "lights out," we all lay in our bunks in silence and the only sounds that could be heard were those of the bugler playing taps and a large fan circulating air down the aisle of the barracks. In my prayer that evening, I confessed to God that I was beginning to hate Airman Jones. I knew it wasn't right to hate someone, but when it came to Jones, I did. My prayer went something like this, "God, I know I should not feel this way, so if you could help me with my bunkmate, I would appreciate it. I can't seem to do anything right in his eyes, no matter how hard I try. So do whatever you can with him."

The next morning, it was like I had died and gone to heaven. Unlike the other mornings which had started off with a barrage of his name-calling, Jones and I started to kid around and enjoy the tasks that were before us. We made our bunks, and soon we were outside and in time for reveille. So it went for the rest of our basic training experience. No name-calling, no confrontation, just working together to accomplish our tasks and duties.

I don't know what God did to Airman Jones to cause such changes overnight, but the difference was like night and day. I knew it was not due to anything I had said or done to him. But, it was an amazing experience! I had never seen anyone change that quickly. That first evening my prayer was one of thankfulness with the assurance that my trip with Uncle Sam would be one with God's presence beside me and within me. That was a comforting discovery for a young man away from home in a foreign land (Texas) and a hostile environment (drill instructors).

I think we all might know someone we think is never going to change no matter what. I suppose with that in mind, we somehow feel our efforts would be in vain. Another point is we don't see ourselves as agents of change for someone else's life. We either think we are not the right person or there is someone else who could do it better. Maybe, we are the one chosen to bring about change in the person's life. As the good book says, "With God, all things are possible." I am reminded of Saint Augustine in his confessions recalling that if it had not been for his mother's prayers, he would never have discovered his destiny in life. Perhaps, we give up on family and friends too soon! Maybe, part of our problem is we don't know what to say. In my case, it was what I did not say that made a difference in Airman Jones' life.

We seem to find in a variety of folks things we don't like about them. I believe what God calls us to do is not to change the person, but to continue to be the person we know God wants us to be and leave the change to God. The challenge is to let God determine our response and not the person confronting us. You may be surprised what God can do with your life.

While in New England doing some work for my denomination, I ran into a couple of bikers who invited me to their home. They both had beards and tattoos up and down their arms and looked rather rugged to me. With some fear and trembling, I went to their place where there were a lot more bikers. They offered me a place on the sofa and asked me what a Southern boy like me was doing in New England. I told them I was working with a local church out of Oakdale trying to get people to know about the love of God. One of the big, burly bikers looked at me and proclaimed, "You're one of us; didn't you read the logo on our backs? It says, 'Bikers for Jesus.'"

Holy Cow! I was among a bunch of "Jesus freaks"! We talked, laughed, and shared stories of our work of ministry. An hour or so went by and finally I had to leave, but I left with more than I came with. The bikers had blessed my life. I went to their home planning on giving them a blessing and went away with more blessings than I could imagine.

Just remember, God uses all people and in some way or another. He is in every human life. Therefore, the most important thing we have to give another person is our friendship. Looking back on my experience with Airman Jones and the Bikers for Jesus, I wouldn't change a thing.

Can you embrace all of God's people?

39

The Chase!

I was just cruising along in my MR2 Spyder with the top down and enjoying the fresh cool air on a September evening! It had been a very enjoyable day visiting a number of my cousins whom I seldom get to see. Kay, my cousin who lives in a small community in western North Carolina called "Pea Ridge," had invited us all to meet at her home for some good Southern cooking and a lot of fellowship. When we all get around the table, it seems as though time just flies. Before I knew it, it was time to get on my way back to Hickory. Normally, that is about an hour-and-a-half drive, but not tonight.

There are a few choices available for traveling from Pea Ridge to Hickory. One would be to take the route through the small community of Ruth on Highway 64 to I-40 in Morganton. The other route would take me south toward Shelby and then north through the community of Casar. The local residents had intended to name the community "Caesar," but had misspelled the word on the form they sent to Raleigh. For some reason, I decided to make my way through Casar and then on to Hickory.

Casar is a community that has not changed much in the last 50 years. It is the place where my wife's father, Wayne Newton, grew up. Also, I had served there as pastor at Zoar Baptist Church over a period of three years. I had gone to the church just out of seminary and got to know many of the folks throughout the community. So I knew most of the roads in the area and felt okay about traveling through the community.

As I passed by Howard Newton's gas and grocery store, I remembered the bologna sandwiches I made there when I was visiting my parishioners in the area. At the back of the store was a long slab of bologna that you cut to the thickness you wanted, then added either mayonnaise or mustard and some cheese to it. Make your own sandwich was a hit with me as it was with many of the Zoar community residents.

On the other side of Casar, I came upon a pick-up truck traveling in the same direction. I maintained a safe distance in my MR2 Spyder until, for some reason, the truck pulled over to the side of the road and stopped. I moved out into the other lane to give the driver room to safely exit from the truck. As I continued my way down the road, I looked back to see the truck was on the road again.

That caused a red flag to go up in my mind. What was that person doing? I felt a little threatened that the truck was now behind me, so I decided to put a little distance between the truck and me. The faster I went, the faster the truck went! So I decided to turn down a road not normally taken, but the truck continued to follow me. So I took another road not normally taken only to discover the truck was still behind me.

Eventually, I pulled in behind a convenience store located in the Vale community. By then it was dark. I sat there for about 15 to 20 minutes before I went into the store. Although I had pastored a church in that community, I wasn't sure where I was at the time because I had gone down so many roads. I soon discovered I was on a main highway that led toward home. I felt a little better about my situation just knowing my location.

The truck with the bright red and white lights on top was nowhere to be seen. The coast was clear! I had given him the slip! So, off I went down Highway 10 toward Hickory and home. Passing an old gas station that had been closed for years, I looked back to see a truck pulling out onto the road behind me again. The bright red and white lights on top of the cab were a dead giveaway. That was the truck that had been following me for the last hour or so.

Now things were getting serious! *What does this person want with me?* I wondered. So again, I felt like the hare in Francis Thompson's poem, "The Hound of Heaven." It seemed there was no way I could escape from this person. I eventually made my way over to Interstate 40 with the truck about a half-mile behind me. I took the 321 South exit and then the 127 exit into Mountain View and home.

The whole experience left me dumbfounded as to what had just taken place. I assumed whoever was driving the truck was planning to do something to me for whatever reason. I had no clue what that might be. The chase had taken on a life-or-death aspect for me. If that person had caught up with me, I don't think it would have gone well for me. I believe the driving force behind his actions was his anger at me.

For sure, there are some folks in the world we need to stay clear of and not get in their way. There are some people in our world who hurt others for no particular reason. Someone once said we need to keep our friends close and our enemies even closer. The point is to know who and where our enemies are in order to keep an eye on them.

Remember the story of David found in First Samuel which describes his rise to prominence after his start as a lowly shepherd? Like Davie Crockett, who killed a bear when he was only three, David killed a giant when he was only a boy. Soon after that, he joined King Saul's army and as the song went, while Saul had killed his thousands, David had killed his tens of thousands. Saul was jealous, so he set in motion plans to get rid of this upstart warrior who was making the king look bad.

The race was on! It seemed no matter what plans King Saul put in place, David was one step ahead of him. Saul's son, Absalom, kept David informed about his father's plans. With this inside help, David was able to escape again and again from the king.

When we become obsessed with thoughts of revenge, and we allow our anger to consume our thoughts, it soon develops into a much more serious problem.

The violence we see and experience in our world is motivated by fear and anger. The writer of the Book of Ephesians instructs us to claim our anger and not let it cause us to sin. It is what we do with our anger that makes the big difference. We have a choice in the matter. We may deny our anger, which will impact us and others around us in a negative way. Denied anger goes nowhere! It just lies around and festers within us. Since we are not ready to face up to the source of our anger, we often take it out on someone else. That is why the writer of Ephesians further instructs us to not let our anger spend the night with us. The longer we keep it around, the more damage it causes.

On the other hand, when we claim our anger, we enable ourselves to process it in a positive way. How do you process anger in a positive way? In his Sermon on the Mount, Jesus told His audience that instead of hating their enemies they needed to love them by forgiving them for what they had done. This is not rocket science stuff, but a simple solution to being at peace with ourselves and with our world.

What are you doing with your anger?

40

The Drive-In Theater

It was Saturday night, and we were off to the drive-in theater located between Spindale and Forest City, North Carolina. Once you paid at the entrance gate, you simply parked your car at one of the outside speakers which hung on five-foot poles. You then rolled your window down and hooked the speaker on it. The speaker and case together were about four inches by five inches and weighed about one pound. There was no stereo at the time, so all movies were in mono, but we had never heard stereo sound, so we didn't miss it.

I can't remember what was showing that night, but I do remember my father's sister, Mildred, went with us. As was the usual custom, the theater showed a double feature each Saturday night with an intermission in between. That was the perfect time to go to the snack bar, so off my aunt and I went. With a good load of popcorn, candy, and drinks, we headed back toward the car. Upon finding our car, we opened the back doors and climbed in.

I looked at my Aunt Mildred with a puzzled expression. Something was missing! Where were Mom and Dad? They had been here when we left, but where were they now? The answer to our question came sooner than we expected. From the front seat, we heard the sounds of a couple who were totally oblivious of us. They did not hear us get into the car, and I don't think they heard us when we left. We had gotten into the wrong car. The car looked like ours! It was a four-door car, and our car had four doors. It looked like our 1952 gray Chevrolet, but it was not our car. We were fooled by the similarities.

Some things are not what they appear to be! The Apostle Paul was concerned about some of his converts who had drifted off and joined another religious group. Perhaps, the new group looked like their former group in a number of ways, such as worship and scripture, and they, too, talked about God. So, what was the big deal? For Paul, it was that the central figure of the other group's faith was not the Christ of faith.

In the Book of Acts 4: 12, Peter delivered his sermon concerning the Christ of faith. In his sermon, Peter told his audience: "In none other is there salvation: for there is no other name under heaven given among men and women by whom we must be saved." (Paraphrase by RLF) For the Apostles Peter and Paul, it did matter very much which chariot they hooked their horses to. The litmus test for these two men was that Christ would be the center of worship and faith.

Just as there were many other religious groups in the early years of Christianity, such is the case today. Not too many years ago, there was a gentleman by the name of the Reverend Jim Jones who led a number of people down a dead-end road. His personality allowed him to take control of their lives. With him, there was no freedom of expression. He controlled the way they dressed, their relationships with family and, most important, their relationship with him, which could be described as being on the sick side of life.

There are some litmus tests we should apply to the various persons who seek to influence our lives. One, does the person seek to liberate me to do what I feel God is calling me to do rather than telling me what I should do with my life? Two, does the person encourage me to go into the world to make a difference or do he/she try to isolate me from family, friends, and community? Three, does the person equip me to be in charge of my life, or does he/she seek to control my life?

Back in the 1970s there was a folk gospel group who went by the name "Love Song." One of the songs on their album was called "Front Seat, Back Seat Driver." A similar song today by Carrie Underwood is "Jesus, Take the Wheel." The point that both songs attempt to convey is that it makes all the difference in the world who's at the wheel.

Who is in the driver's seat of your life?

41

The House on the Hill

When I grew up in Grace Cotton Mill Village in western North Carolina in the 40s and 50s, it was easy to identify which families were the most prominent by the size of their houses. There was one large colonial house that had huge columns on the front, as well as a grand staircase that led to the upstairs. Although I had never been inside this home, on a few occasions I had been at the front door promoting my shoeshine business. For me, this was an impressive place, as well as it should have been, because it was the home of the plant supervisor.

As I walked down the road, the houses became much smaller, but they were still much larger than the house I lived in. The next three large houses were the homes of the first-, second-, and third-shift supervisors. Farther down the road were the homes of the mill hands. This was where my home was located.

If I thought I had seen a big house in the mill village, I had seen nothing like the largest house in North Carolina. Those of us who live in western North Carolina are privileged to be able to travel a short way to see the grandeur of this great, stately home built during the late 1800s. The Biltmore House in Asheville was built by the Vanderbilt family and was occupied in the early twentieth century. Today, it is a renowned tourist attraction.

In light of the above, it is interesting to note what Jesus said about homes and the future of God's people. In the Gospel according to John, Jesus told His disciples about His Father's house: "In My Father's house are many mansions (rooms); if it were not so, I would have told you. I go to prepare a place for you. And if I go and prepare a place for you, I will come again and receive you to myself; that where I am, there you may be also." John 14: 1-3 (Paraphrase by RLF)

A popular interpretation of this passage of scripture is that Jesus spoke of some future place and time where/when there will be no more homelessness. All of God's people will have a place to stay! That place is no shack, for Jesus calls it a "mansion." It is a place that has been prepared for us. The first home of Jesus was located in a stable where the smells of animals were evident everywhere. We are told there was no room in the inn for Him and His parents. Later on, as an adult, He told those who followed Him, He had no place to lay His head.

Where, then, are those mansions? Like the locations featured in the movies of "Star Trek" and "Star Wars," their location is in a world far, far away. But, what if such a mansion is not as far away as we might suppose, but in a place closer by? What if instead of being in a place somewhere far away from us, it is a place within us. Perhaps, in our deeper soul! Is this not the place the Christ of faith wishes to occupy? Consider the words from the Book of Revelation: "Behold, I stand at your life's door and knock. If you would open the door, I would like to come inside and have fellowship with you." Revelation 3: 20 (Paraphrase by RLF)

Since death is the beginning of new life, the historical Jesus envisioned His resurrected life as having no limits of time or space. In the resurrected life, He became the universal Christ. In this new life He meets us not from the outside, but calls us to meet Him on the inside. To find Him, we must go inside ourselves into our Holy of Holies. As the Christ of faith, He is always where He needs to be and calls us to come join Him in his new life.

I believe the metaphor mansion describes the elevated life, which has truly been provided and is available to all of God's people in the present moment. Therefore, to speak of mansions is to speak of our liberation into the new life of Christ. In our world today, mansions are a symbol of division between the people who have and the people who have not a place to lay their head, which is similar to how Jesus came into the world. They are symbols of wealth, power, and fame. It is all a matter of which side of the tracks you live on. Therefore, when we attempt to see the world through the eyes of God, we see how equal we all are, not how divided we are. We discover through the eyes of God, we come from the same source of life. All life comes from God and all life returns to God.

A favorite song of some of my relatives is "Cabin on the Hill." For many years every time the Skipper family got together that song was sure to be sung around the piano. Whether it's a cabin or mansion on the hill doesn't matter. It is where God meets and gathers His people. It is where God builds His home.

The Book of Revelation speaks of streets of gold, which means to me that the most valuable element on earth, which the financial world is based on, has no great value in the coming reality of God. While I'm not all that sure as to what the coming eschatology (fullness of time) will look like, I concur with the gospel song, "He Lives," I know He lives, because He lives in the deepest recesses of my soul.

The Apostle Paul wrote in First Corinthians that we are the temple of God (the house of God, or might we say the mansion of God). If this be true, then we are the place Christ seeks to prepare for God. It is we, not God who need work.

What shape is your house in?

42

The Mysterious Casket

It was mid-summer in the small town located about 20 miles southwest of Topeka, Kansas. The 1950 heat wave was in full force with temperatures soaring above the 100-degree mark. An air conditioning was very scarce at this time in this particular area. The best you could do was open the doors and windows with screens and let the wandering wind blow through. In spite of all attempts, there was very little escape from the blistering heat.

On this particular day, Sam Wilson from the funeral home in Topeka was traveling to the home of the McFarland's to check on Mr. McFarland, who had died a few days before. The funeral was being delayed a bit so some family and friends living some distance away could have time to arrive. Sam was just doing a routine check to ensure the makeup applied to Mr. McFarland's face was still in place and to see if the family needed anything else.

As was the custom in those days, there was a vigil in the home while the body lay in state. As different members of the community came and went at various times during the day, there was always someone there to greet them. As Sam entered the home in the early morning day of the funeral, he made his way over to the casket. Looking down into the casket, he was shocked by what he saw. He wondered what had happened here. Had someone back at the funeral home made a great mistake? Surely not.

Just then, he heard voices coming from the kitchen. Making his way down the hall, he soon arrived at the door and stood there in silence for a few seconds. There were several members of the family and some friends drinking coffee and reminiscing of days gone by. Sam cleared his voice to get their attention. A voice from the back rang out, "Good morning, Sam. How are you doing today?"

"Well, huh, ok I guess! I just came by to check on the family, and as I passed by the casket in the living room, I huh, I noticed that, huh, that Mr. McFarland was not in the casket."

"Oh, yes!" One of the family members spoke up. "We were sitting around last night, and Leroy reminded us we had never had a family portrait made like we had talked about for so many years. So, we got Dad out of the casket and stood him up with all of us around and Carl took the picture. Only problem, we couldn't get him back in the casket, so we laid him across the bed."

It would have been nice if Mr. McFarland could have been alive at the time, but that wasn't the case. The McFarland family had plans, but had just never gotten around to carrying them out. Time had run out on them, and now it was too late to have the family portrait they had talked about for so many years. There seemed to be many excuses why the family never got together for a picture. Well, since everybody will be here Thanksgiving or maybe Christmas, or maybe even New Year's Day, we will wait until then. One excuse after another had finally led to the family's current situation.

Procrastination! That is the use of delayed action on something that could be done in the present moment. It seems that every time we make plans to do something positive, something else gets in our way. That something that keeps getting in our way often leads us away from our good intent. Having good intentions is not the goal, but putting our good intentions into action is the goal.

I once had a parishioner who never came to any of our church services. When our paths crossed at times, he would tell me he intended to be at church the coming Sunday. In the beginning, I would tell him that was good and I looked forward seeing him on Sunday. Of course, he never came! So I devised a new tactic. The next time our paths crossed and we had the same conversation as before, instead of giving him my blessings on his good intent, I called him a liar. My response to him was, "You know and I know and God knows that deep down you have absolutely no intention of being at church this coming Sunday." The next Sunday he was at church.

Someone has said, "The road to hell is filled with a lot of folks' good intentions." The Gospel according to Mark tells us we all have a certain amount of time on the face of the earth, and we do not know exactly when our time is up. In light of that, we should live each day as though it is our last. Each day, renew our relationship with our Lord and do all the good we can do. Re-connect with broken relationships. Right the wrongs we have done to others. Speak positive words to one another. Be open to God's calling upon our lives.

Is procrastination a part of your life?

43

The Times! They Are A Changing

It was one of those days when my mother was so sick with a migraine headache she could not get out of bed. Eventually, my father called the doctor's office for help. I can't remember how long it took, but at some point the doctor showed up at our door. He carried a small black bag with his medical supplies and other instruments of healing. Generally, he gave my mother a shot of some sort, and later on her migraine would go away. I can remember other occasions when the doctor came to our home. At the age of seven, I came down with rheumatic fever. During my three months of bed rest, he came to our home regularly to check on me.

The unique visit by the family doctor has just about gone away. It has been replaced by EMS. We no longer call the doctor's office, but 911. At one time, in small towns the funeral home hearse functioned in the dual role of carrying the dead to the church and graveyard and also carrying emergency victims to the hospital. We now hear the sounds of the EMS vehicle going up and down the highway to pick up and deliver patients to local emergency rooms. Today, the local fire department is the first responder to emergency situations.

Also, in years gone by, it was the custom of family practice doctors to make visits to the hospital to see patients. Now, a group of doctors within the hospital known as "hospitalists" do the daily visits to patients, which frees up the local family practice doctors to see more patients in their offices.

It is true: "They don't do it like they used to!" Change is always taking place in the world around us. In his book, *The Christ of Culture*, H. R. Niebuhr described how Jesus brought new ways of looking at God into his Jewish culture. Like us, many of the people did not like the changes

He was suggesting. They could not understand how God could be the way Jesus described. The Sermon on the Mount was just too radical for them.

Social and religious change comes slowly. There is the story about a small church in the wildwood where every Sunday as the congregation was leaving one little elderly lady would take the preacher's hand and say, "Fine sermon today." One Sunday he chose as his sermon topic, "The Danger of Tobacco." He covered the subject matter from cigarettes to dipping snuff and challenged his congregation to reconsider their use of this substance. That Sunday when this elderly lady greeted the minister, she was overheard to say, "You've gone from preaching to meddling now preacher!" His message did not suit her lifestyle, because dipping snuff was a habit that had been handed down from generation to generation in her family and she was not about to give it up at this late date in her life. As they say, "No good deed goes unpunished."

Jesus often warned his followers not to conform to the ways of the world, but to be conformed to the Kingdom of God. Now, that bit of advice is open for a variety of interpretations. Some people, like the Amish, have removed themselves from the communities around them. They have in times past refused to use the modern conveniences. Women wore their hair long, and their dresses covered their legs. There is nothing wrong with this lifestyle. They lived a good, wholesome life.

In New England, there was a group of folks that became known as "The Shakers." They, too, isolated themselves from the general public. In their worship services, the men and women did not sit together. I suppose they thought if they did it might cause the men to have some lustful thoughts during worship. It must have worked; the whole group died out years ago.

An issue still in some debate today is the use of makeup by women. In Biblical days it was a sign of loose morals. Today, that is still the case in a number of faith groups. I have friends who refuse to have a TV set in the house or go to the movies. The list goes on and on! They struggle with the question, "What part of the world must I avoid and what part of the world must I keep?"

It is an issue we must decide for ourselves. The Apostle Paul spoke at length of food offered to idols. He personally did not have any problem eating food offered to idols, because idols were empty of any power to impact one's life. Therefore, idols were nothing but an object. But many believers of that day thought it would cause great harm for them to see other believers eating food that had been offered to an idol. Paul goes on to say that although he had no problem with eating food offered to idols, he would not eat such food if it would cause another believer to stumble.

This stumbling issue is not a big deal among modern Christians. Some years ago it was not the custom of a man and woman to live together without being married. Today the numbers are fairly equal among Christians and non-Christians who practice this living arrangement. It's just not a big deal anymore with the general public. Today, the relationship of two men or two women living together as husband and wife is becoming more and more accepted as normal behavior.

As we continue through the 21st century, we will see more and more changes in what is accepted by our culture. Dr. Karl Menninger wrote a book many years ago entitled, *Whatever Became of Sin*? Good question! The words of Bob Dylan come to mind, "The times, they are changing."

Perhaps the word "sin" needs to be updated in order to have relevance for today's world. If what the world offers us is detrimental to our health and well-being, then it should not be allowed to be a part of our lives. In addition to this, we should not allow cultural change to cause damage to our spiritual well-being. Of course, spirituality is a whole can of worms. Martin Buber in his book, *I and Thou*, states spirituality begins with our relationship with the world around us. It is in the meeting of our fellow earthlings that the possibility of discovering who we are and for what reason we have been created. Spirituality is concerned with our destiny and our purpose in life.

This is where the world of electronics works against us. A friend of mine, Hayden Howell, sent me some photos of some young adults on a tour bus in London, England. As the bus passed the Tower of Big Ben all those in the group were busy working with their cell phones. If there were an "I – Thou" moment to be experienced, they missed it. Perhaps, we too miss out on the deeper experiences of life that surround us because we are looking somewhere else.

Yes, the times they are changing and so are we.

Are you being changed for better or worse?

44

The Way It Was

Spending the summer on my grandparents' farm in western North Carolina in the early 1950s was a unique experience. Water had to be drawn from a well, and at night oil lamps provided light throughout the house. When I needed to go to the bathroom during the day, I had to walk about 200 feet down a pathway leading from the house to an outside toilet known as an "out house." At nighttime the bedpan, which was tucked away under the bed, was available for use.

The open fireplace was always going until the late evening hours when everyone was in bed. It was by this old fireplace I sat with Grandma as she combed out her long hair and braided it. It was grandma/grandson time! She told stories of long ago when she grew up. It was a good feeling for me to be in her presence. I felt safe and accepted.

The three favorite times of the day for me were breakfast, lunch, and supper. The whole family sat around the large rectangular table as the conversation flowed in all directions. It was one of those times when you didn't know exactly what was being discussed, but it felt good being there anyway.

During the day, I went out in the fields to help plant potato slips. At other times, you would find my Aunt Joyce and me climbing an apple tree. Some days, we would go over to the sugarcane patch for a sweet treat. Watermelons were always in abundance in a field near the farmhouse.

Some days I would go over near the barn were my Grandpa Skipper was making molasses. A mule provided the horsepower to turn the gears that extracted the juice to make candy from the molasses which was a great treat.

WALKING IN GRANDPA'S FOOTSTEPS: STORIES OF GOD'S GRACE AND MERCY

On one occasion, a neighbor's barn needed some repairs. About a dozen men from the community got together and repaired the barn. There was no payment for the work; it was just what neighbors did for one another. Each person knew if and when they needed help, the community would be there for them.

Although the small farm life has just about disappeared in our part of the world, that is, western North Carolina, it still holds some very important truths for all of us. One, in the day-to-day routine of life, everyone has something to give for the well-being of the family. Two, as part of a greater community, the family has something to give for the well-being of the community. These acts of kindness gave expression to how we are all connected to one another.

The "Simple Life" is the connected life. In a song years ago, the words informed us that "people who need people are the most blessed people in the world." It is in our acts of kindness that we begin to discover our capacity to bless and be blessed. From a Biblical point of view, that is what it means to be human.

Scriptures tell us Jesus hardly owned anything. No house, no donkey, no land, just the clothes on his back and the sandals on his feet. The men he had gathered around him had some special skills, so he didn't go hungry. I suppose Mary, Martha, and Lazarus, his good friends, saw to it he had clothes to wear.

One of the songs by the Beatles is "I Get by with a Little Help from My Friends." The people we have around us play a role in how we live out life. In his book, *No Man Is an Island*, Thomas Merton wrote that a life worth living is the life that is given away. He goes on to say in order to do that; we must rebel against ourselves, for it is the "self" that gets in our way of doing what we need to do.

God created us to be in community with all people, and it is only in a loving and caring community we discover the true meaning and purpose of our lives. We are still learning how to do this. From the news I receive on a daily basis, it seems we still have a long way to go.

Has your life become too complicated?

45

Tipping Over Canoes

I had been in the Boy Scouts for about a year, and it was the summer of 1957. The most exciting thing that was happening that summer was Boy Scout Camp at Lake Lanier, near Tryon, North Carolina. Our home for the week would consist of a small, one-room cabin with roll-up sides and bunk beds. Each cabin had a senior scout assigned to it. Lucky me! My first cousin, Harold Ellenburg, was our scout leader.

Each day, we signed up for the various activities that were offered. I had heard the canoeing trip out on the lake was a lot of fun, so I signed up for that activity. The canoe was large enough to accommodate 13 scouts, with one being a senior scout who insured we were going in the right direction. As we tried to sync our oars, our canoe went zig-zigging across the lake. Eventually, we got pretty good at that oaring business as we picked up speed. Everything was going along just great as we made our way back into the docking area, when all of a sudden several smaller canoes on our left and right started to pull in front of us. Those of us located up front did the only thing we knew to do to protect ourselves; we started to tip over the other canoes with our oars. Boy Scouts in those canoes went sprawling in all directions. From the dock, we heard the camp supervisors blowing their whistles trying to get us to stop, but it was all to no avail. We just kept tipping over the canoes until we had completed our mission. When everything was said and done, we had tipped over about five or six canoes, that then found a way to the bottom of Lake Lanier.

Everyone in our canoe was condemned to solitary confinement. We had to stay in our cabins for the remainder of the day or risk being sent back home. Oh, Lord, I didn't want that to happen, so I carried out my sentence to the nth degree. Back home I was known as a troublemaker among some of my family's friends and relatives. I didn't want to prove them right and have to endure the punishment my parents would inflict on me. So, for the rest of the week I was the best-behaved Boy Scout at the camp.

I can't remember if I told my parents about the incident or not, but knowing me, I probably didn't. There was no need to cause any more stress on them than need be. Trouble seemed to be my middle name, but it was no one's fault but my own. It seemed I had gotten rather good at making bad choices. I walked to the beat of a different drummer, and it had gotten me into a lot of trouble.

One late evening, when the sun had long run its course across the Galilean sky, the disciples of Jesus were out on the Sea of Galilee, when all of a sudden, a storm came upon them. Their boat (canoe) started to take on water and began to rock back and forth. It looked as though they were going down, but in the distance they could see Jesus coming to them walking on the water. As He got closer to the boat, Peter asked if he might join Him out on the water and permission was granted. At first Peter was doing okay, but the storm distracted him and he began to sink. At that point, Jesus took Peter's hand and lifted him up out of the swirling waters and helped him back into the boat.

Our senior pastor at First Baptist Hickory, Phillip Reynolds, in one of his sermons informed us we need to be content where the Lord has placed us. It is the right place to be for the time and situation we are facing. But, regardless of where the Lord places us, we are allowed to go somewhere else if we so choose. He won't stop us.

Being where our Lord has placed us does not mean turmoil cannot come our way. It certainly can! You might have some idiot like me tip over your canoe. In spite of the storms that might blow upon your life, He can still come to us and bring into our lives a sense of peace and calmness.

Are you content where our Lord has placed you?

46

Two Red Shirts

It was an exciting time for me getting ready for the upcoming school year in the eighth grade at Fairforest Junior High. Mom always took me shopping for new clothes. That generally meant I got new shoes, a couple pair of jeans, and a couple of shirts. Red was my favorite color, so I ended up with two red shirts. The shirts were very similar, so when I wore one of them one day and the other the next, my classmates asked if I just had one red shirt. I really had not thought too much about it, so the question caught me off guard. The question did embarrass me! I didn't know I was supposed to have more than two shirts for school.

It was the first time in my life someone had made any statement about my clothes. At the other schools I had attended, no one really cared what you wore to school or how many times you wore certain clothes. But, this was not the case in junior high! My red shirts soon became a common joke among my classmates. "Hey, Ford, which shirt are you wearing tomorrow, the red one or the red one?"

I never said anything to my parents about that situation, because I knew they were doing the best they could for me and I didn't want to make them feel bad. At that time, there was not a name for the sort of interaction that I experienced. Today, it is popularly known as "bullying." Although I was never physically attacked, the words from my peers were hurtful. So, my plan of action was to stay as far away from those students as possible. Fighting has never been a big thing with me! For one thing, being as small as I was at the time, it was in my best interest to find another way of dealing with such issues. My normal operating procedure has been to move on and leave behind those who have not liked me for one reason or another.

One day Jesus was speaking of His experience in His home town of Nazareth where it was said, "Is this not Joseph's son, so what's so special about him?" Jesus went on to say a prophet has no honor in his home town or country. Later on, He told His disciples if a town or village would not receive them, they were to shake the dust of that place from their feet and go on to the next place.

It was not that He was giving up on those who did not like Him. He realized at that moment and time, it was time to move on to another place. Sometimes, we need to do the same! Perhaps, on another day and time, we may have an opportunity to make a connection. Perhaps, eventually, those who have not liked us and made fun of us will find the capacity to look beyond our outward appearance. Maybe, at some point in time, they will discover the common ground, rather than just focusing on the differences. Maybe, they will come to see how we are more alike than they first realized.

This thought is found in Genesis 1: 27, where the writer states: "God created human beings in God's image; in the image of God, God created male and female." (Paraphrase by RLF) So, what does it mean to be "created in the image of God" as the writer of the Book of Genesis claims for all humanity? Simply stated, we are all spiritual beings and that includes "the good, the bad, and the ugly" within the human race. It is the spiritual world that gives birth to the physical world and not the other way around. Therefore, our primary essence is spiritual, not physical. That is our connection to one another throughout the world.

In the letter of I John 4: 8, we are informed: "The person who does not love all people, does not know God, for God's love embraces the whole wide world." (Paraphrase by RLF)

Therefore, we may say every human being has the capacity to know and experience God in a personal way and to love as we are loved, to embrace as we are embraced, and to accept as we are accepted. It should not matter to us if the person is rich or poor, but that we are willing to acknowledge we have a connection with every human being in the world. In a way, when we attack another human being, we attack something about ourselves. In attacking others, we detract from our own humanity. Some doctors would say this is partly because we see in the other person what we don't like in ourselves or what we are afraid to face up to in ourselves.

From his Sermon on the Mount, Jesus told his audience: "Whatsoever you want others to do to you, you should do to them." Matthew 7: 12 (Paraphrase by RLF)

Are you willing to embrace those whom God embraces?

47

Which Way Should I Go?

It was the month of December as we made our way into the mountains of eastern Tennessee. This would be a pleasant ride from Hickory, North Carolina, on I-40 West, and in a few hours we would be in downtown Gatlinburg and Pigeon Forge. That had become an annual trip for us, so we were familiar with the terrain. We had a GPS system in our car, but since we were going into familiar territory there was no need to use it. Cruising through the mountains on a beautiful fall day, what could go wrong? Eventually, I asked the question, "Are we on the right road?"

The response from my co-pilot was, "Yes, I remember this road!" After driving another 30 minutes or more, we were on what we thought was our downhill descent into Gatlinburg. Around a sharp curve and up another small incline and the unthinkable happened— the road ran out.

We sat there looking into a deep, wooded forest and thinking, "How did this happen?" Like a Rod Serling episode of "Twilight Zone," we were on a road to nowhere. In a situation like that there is only one choice: we turned the car around and went back the same way we came in. As we retraced our journey, we wondered what had happened. Where did we go wrong?

Eventually, we found the right road that led to our destination. So I began to wonder, "How many times have I been down a road that came to a dead end?" At one point in my life, I thought God wanted me to be an insurance salesman. I was working with WSPA –TV in Spartanburg, South Carolina, at the time and trying to sort through what God wanted me to do. When I came home from work one day, my mother told me a local insurance company had called and wanted to talk to me about working for them. It struck a chord! That was what I had been praying about, and now God had answered my prayer. I called the insurance company and set up an appointment to go in for an interview. The interview went great! I had come highly recommended for the job and after interviewing me, they were sure I was the right person.

All I had to do now was to have a physical, and I would be on my way into the insurance business. I had just finished a four-year tour of duty with the Air Force, so I knew I was in good shape. At the doctor's office, after a number of tests were performed, the doctor came to talk with me. The news was a startling surprise to me. I had failed the physical. But, how could that be? What had gone so wrong for me? Didn't they know this was what God was calling me to do?

It seems the doctor had heard a murmur while listening to my heart. Also, the EKG showed some unusual activity that confirmed I had a defective valve in my heart. He asked me point blank, "Have you ever had rheumatic fever?" I knew I had, but I told him a lie that day.

"What's rheumatic fever?" I asked, trying to play the village idiot. Well, the results were sent back to the company headquarters. A few days later, I got a phone call from the vice president of human resources informing me they could not hire me with my current physical condition.

I continued by work with WSPA-TV and eventually the thought of going into a full-time Christian vocation came to me. But, that presented several problems. First of all, I am an introvert, which means getting up before a group of people to do anything is very difficult for me. One of the things I hated most about high school was the oral book report. I would do almost anything to get out of delivering it before my classmates, whom I had known for a long time. Secondly, I had just barely escaped high school. I was a C student, at best. In fact, I had to take physical education as a senior, which was not required of seniors, so I would have enough credits to graduate. So, the thought of going off to college was foreign to me. If I had barely made it in high school, how was I ever going to make it in collage?

I had gone to Spartanburg Technical College out of high school and barely made it through a two-year course in electronic technology, so why would I think I could do any better now? That was my litmus test for God. I would take the SAT, which determines something about your ability to do college work, and if I did well enough to get into college, I would accept God's call for me to go into full-time ministry.

So, on a late fall Saturday morning, I went to the elementary school on South Church Street in Spartanburg, South Carolina, to take the test. At the time, I did not know there were books you could study to prepare you to take the test. After taking the test, I left the building not knowing if my test scores would be high enough or not. About a week or so later, my SAT score finally came back, and it was 1170 which, unknown to me, was good enough to get me into most colleges. The test score was also sent to Spartanburg Methodist College, and I was much surprised when the college called to let me know I had been accepted.

Yes, I have been on several roads that led to nowhere, but God has always been there to guide me back onto the right highway. I have come to see dead ends not as a failure, but as a challenge. Dead ends allow us to evaluate where we have been and where we need to go. In fact, we could say there is no such thing as failure, only opportunities. These opportunities help us learn from our dead-end adventures.

Back in his days as a Jewish scholar, Saul set out on a trip from Jerusalem to Antioch to arrest and punish a group of those so-called "Christians." A bright light and a voice only he could hear and see stopped him dead in his tracks. The voice called out his name, "Saul, Saul, why do you seek to persecute me?" That encounter is often called Paul's conversion experience. Whatever you might call it, Paul did a U-turn. His life took a different direction.

In the story, "Alice in Wonderland," Alice comes to a crossroads and does not know which way to go. Nearby sits a Cheshire cat, to whom she asks the question, "Which way should I go?"

In response, the Cat asked, "Where do you want to go?"

Alice replied, "I don't know!"

The cat then replied, "It doesn't matter then!"

When we are attempting to follow God's will for our life, and we encounter roadblocks or dead ends, God will either remove it or show us another way to go. If God calls us, He will make a way for us.

Have you been down any dead-end roads lately?

48

Why God Made Dogs!

The picture on the mantel showed a little boy perhaps three or four years old holding a small, white dog. From that point on, dogs continued to be a part of the Ford family household. Some years later, Buster, a Boston terrier, made his way into the Ford family. Soon after that we took in Betty, a 12-year-old cocker spaniel. She adopted Buster as her own and disciplined him if he went near the road. The discipline consisted of grabbing Buster by the nap of the neck and giving him a good shake. It worked! Buster stayed away from the road after a few doses of that.

Later in life when I started my own home, my family lived in the parsonage of Mt. Vernon Baptist Church. We were located on highway 10 in Vale, North Carolina, which proved to be the perfect spot for stray dogs. Laddy, a collie that looked like he had traveled 40 miles of bad road, came to our door. He was filthy, his hair all tangled and a gash across his nose. After Gail, my wife, washed him and combed him and provided food for him, he looked like Lassie. I'm told that Lassie was a male dog, not a female.

Later on, as we were returning from a trip to Hickory, we passed a restaurant on Highway 10. Out in front of the restaurant was a dog that was only skin and bones. We passed by and went on home, but Gail was determined to go back and give the dog something to eat. There was no stopping her, so I went along. The owner of the restaurant came out and told us she would like to get the dog away from her restaurant. It seemed the dog was bad for business. So we piled him into our 1978 Monza and took him home. After some tender loving care from Gail, the dog regained his weight and looked good as new.

Later on, we moved to Mountain View, a community a few miles down the road from Hickory, North Carolina. We were off the beaten path, so you would think dealing with stray dogs would not be a problem, but not so. These homeless canines seemed to know how to find us. Scruffy was a neighborhood nuisance. We eventually took him in and with some tender loving care from my wife, the dog was soon looking as good as new. His death many years later was devastating to our family.

In addition to Scruffy, Gail found a small dog on the side of the road and named him Dexter. Our daughter, Lauran, brought home a beagle-looking dog that we named Eva. In addition to the dogs, we took in a stray cat.

One summer, Eva became sick, and within a few weeks I sat beside her and held her paw as she took her last breath. Two weeks later Dexter died, and I was there with him to hold his paw as he took his last breath. I cried more for those animals than I did when my own parents died. Those animals had touched my soul! They taught me how to love unconditionally. I could scold them, and they would come right back to me with their tails wagging. They never held a grudge against me and loved me, whether I had been good to them or not. They never dwelt on my bad side, but just saw the good in me that I often could not see for myself.

So, why did God make dogs?

The answer is a simple one!

To teach us how to be human!

49

Your Arms Are Too Short

An open invitation was sent out to all the classrooms at Ruth Elementary School: anyone interested being in the school band needed to come to the activity room. So, when the day came, I was ready! My favorite TV show at the time was "Howdy Doody" with Buffalo Bob and Clarabell, who later would go on to become Captain Kangaroo. The latter character played a trombone on the show, so that was the musical instrument I wanted to play.

At the activity room, I stood in line waiting for my opportunity. Wow! This would be a dream come true! Imagine me playing the same musical instrument as Clarabell. That was a chance of a lifetime, and I couldn't believe it was happening to me. I didn't know first-graders were allowed to make that much noise.

Eventually, it came my turn to declare what instrument I would like to play. "I would like to play the trombone," was my response.

Then I heard the most devastating words I had ever heard, "Your arms are too short! Next!" Boy, those weren't the words I wanted to hear! How devastating it was for a first-grader to hear those words. So, I went back to my classroom downhearted and disappointed.

That was one of many occasions I was told I did not have the talent to do what I was seeking to do. Later on in my school life, I was not fast enough to be on the track team; not strong enough to be on the football team; not tall enough to be on the basketball team; not good enough to be on the baseball team! One dead-end street after another! What might God have been trying to say to me at that point and time in my life? Maybe, it was God's way of saying to me, "Bob, don't waste your time on something I have not given you gifts to do. There will be other things I will have for you to do, things I have given you talents and the ability to accomplish."

So, I found other outlets that allowed me to accomplish some of my dreams. I made the basketball team at the local Salvation Army in spite of being short in stature, and I became one of the top scorers on the team. I pitched for the Saxton Mill baseball team with the second best win/loss record for the season. While my first choice could not be realized, Plan B worked just fine.

In his letter to the Romans, the Apostle Paul informed the Christian congregation he had intended to visit them, but things kept getting in his way. So, Paul had to revert to Plan B. It was not his first choice, but it was one of his options. He went down the pathway that was available to him. As in the poem by Robert Frost, he took "The Road Not Taken," and it was the road that made all the difference in his advancement of the gospel.

Giving up is the easy thing to do, but continuing the journey of life wherever it may lead is the challenging part of life. While some pathways seem to offer very little reward, they may turn out to be some of the most rewarding experiences in our lives. Discovering what God is doing in our Plan B is discovering something about our destiny in life and what we are capable of doing and becoming.

If you find yourself in a situation in which "Your Arms Are Too Short," try Plan B!

50

The Request

In the process of making my rounds, I had a nurse call me aside to inform me a young man in the Intensive Care Unit (ICU) had requested a visit from the chaplain. Of course, I wanted to know what was going on with him and was told he had serious heart and lung problems and was not expected to live. I believe the young man was around 24 years of age, single but with great family support from two sisters and his mother. The nurse did not know if he had had any pastoral visits from local clergy.

With this bit of information, I made my way to his room, introduced myself, and asked him what was on his mind. At some point in our conversation, the young man said he needed God in his life. I asked him if he had any ideas as to how that happens. To the best of his understanding, he thought it had something to do with going to church. "What is it about church that brings God into your life," I asked?

"I have seen people that talk to the preacher, and they seem to have God in their lives after they do that," was his response

"Do you see them doing this at church?" I inquired.

"When they come forward and the preacher has prayer with them," he answered.

"Is that something you want me to do with you?" I asked.

"Yes, I would like for you to do that," was his response.

"What is it that you would like to say to God?" I asked.

"I don't know, but I guess to save me," he responded.

"And what does it mean for you to be saved?" I asked.

"I'm not sure, but I suppose it has something to do with my sins. I know I'm a sinner, and I need forgiveness. I know I need God in my life and I need a preacher to pray with me," he responded.

"Are there particular sins you need forgiveness for?" I asked.

"Well, I don't go to church like I should, and I don't pray or read my Bible like I should. I drink quite a bit, and I have used some drugs. Also, I cuss a lot at times, but this is only when I'm angry. I believe this is why God is angry with me and doing all these things to me," was his response.

"So you believe you are in the hospital because God is angry with you?" I asked.

"Well, yes, yes I do. Of course, I deserve it! I know a lot of it is what I have done to myself, and now I'm paying the price for the kind of life I have lived. I don't know if I'm going to make it out of the hospital. I have trouble breathing. I'm scared I'm going to die, and I don't want to die. I want you to pray with me so things will be all right. I want to get better and live the kind of life I should have been living. I don't want to die," was his response.

"What scares you about dying," I asked?

"I don't want to go to hell! If I die now, I'll go to hell, and that is not where I want to go. I want to go to heaven, not hell. That's why I need to get closer to God, so He won't send me to hell. Can you help me?" was his response.

At that time, I could see tears flowing down his cheeks. "Tell me about your tears! What are you feeling now that is causing tears to flow down your cheeks?" I asked.

WALKING IN GRANDPA'S FOOTSTEPS: STORIES OF GOD'S GRACE AND MERCY

At that time, there was just silence as he gazed downward. I allowed the silence to continue, just sitting there feeling his hurt and pain.

I remembered the scripture that says, "Be still (silent) and know that I am God." I waited for the young man to respond when he was ready. We just sat there in each other's presence in silence. At the same time, I knew God was present and active through me in order for the young man to know God was present in him. I was in no hurry. I was willing to sit there for as long as it took.

Eventually he spoke! Clearing his throat and wiping a tear or two from his cheeks:

> I know that Jesus has come into my life. I just feel like the Lord has embraced me and I heard him say "I love you" to me. I don't understand what has happened, but I feel closer to God and that God is closer to me. I feel at peace with myself and with God. That's strange, because we didn't even pray. I thought we had to pray for that to happen.

Can you explain that," he asked?

> What if this whole visit has been a prayer to God? What if God has been listening in on our conversation, and all we have said here today has reached the ears of God and He has accepted our conversation as our prayer to Him? You wanted to be closer to God, and He heard you and came closer to you. You confessed your sins and God forgave you. You said you were afraid of going to hell, and God clothed you with His presence. This is heaven! This is God's gift to you, and it is His promise to you that whether you live or die, He will be with you. This is what conversion is all about. It is about discovery. Discovering God is in our lives! Discovering we are forgiven! Discovering God's embrace of our life!

Do you think that has happened to you," I asked?

Again, tears flowed from his eyes making their way down his cheeks to the corner of his mouth. Again silence! Again I waited! I was tempted to hurry things along by breaking the silence, but somehow I resisted. At that time, I felt as though all my energy had withdrawn from me, and I felt weak. I remembered some of the beatitudes that related to what was happening to the young man before me and to me as well:

> Blessed are the poor in spirit (Those that pour out their life so that others might have life), for theirs is the kingdom of heaven.
>
> Blessed are they that mourn: for they shall be comforted!"
>
> Blessed are they which do hunger and thirst after righteousness: for they shall be filled." Matthew 5: 1-2 (Paraphrase by RLF)

These sayings of Jesus from the Sermon on the Mount seemed to identify what was happening before me and to me. Yes, God was at work here in many ways, and I was the one chosen to be His messenger. Here I sat poor in spirit. The young man before me was being comforted and his desire to be made right with God was coming to fruition. I felt tired, but it was a good feeling. I closed my eyes and enjoyed this as though I were sunbathing on a warm spring day. I nearly went to sleep, but caught myself in time before it happened.

Eventually, the young man looked up at me and said:

> This is what I wanted but never seemed to be able to make it happen. I was brought up in a Christian home. My parents and my sisters have told me over and over again I needed to have Jesus in my life, but I just ignored them. But, today is

different. My resistance was gone and I was able to invite the Lord into my life. It was what I needed to do but just could not bring myself to do. It feels good. I feel like I'm a new man now, since my fears about my future have gone from me. Momma always wanted me to be baptized, but I don't guess that can happen now

Again tears flowed from his eyes and silence again returned to the room.

I waited a few moments and then responded:

I can make it happen, if you will accept my form of baptism. While you are unable to get out of bed at this time, I would be willing to baptize you by sprinkling. I have a chaplain's kit in my office. I can set up an altar here in your room. If you would like, I can get your family to come along with your nurses and doctors. Would you be open to that?

He agreed. So, I made plans to perform the baptism the next morning. I informed his nurses about the service and asked them to inform the patient's doctors. I went out into the waiting room to inform the family about my visit with the patient and his wishes to be baptized. They were concerned that only two family members at a time were allowed in the room. I told them the rule was being set aside for the baptismal service. They could all come in at the same time.

The next morning, with the altar set up on the patient's tray and the room full with family, nursing staff, and several doctors, I baptized the young man by placing water on his forehead three times in the name of God the Father, God the Son, and God the Holy Spirit. There wasn't a dry eye in the whole room. It was a touching moment as God poured out His Spirit on all of us.

I asked the patient if he had anything he would like to say. After clearing his throat, he looked up and as his eyes surveyed the room, he thanked everyone for being there.

> I have now found what I have always been looking for but never knew where to find it. I have invited the Lord into my life and to forgive me of my sins. I feel like a great weight has been taken from me, and I want to thank all of you for praying for me and for not giving up on me. You have made a difference in my life.

Two days later the young man died. The family asked me to perform the funeral service, which I was more than willing to do. In that brief time with the patient, I once again was surprised by God. I thought, maybe conversion is not just something that happens at a particular time and date, but is ongoing. Maybe, day by day, we are being converted. So, as I sat in the patient's room, God's presence had come upon both of us, and we both were so afraid. But, we heard God's voice whisper, "Don't be afraid, for 'I Am' with you!" The same God who discovered Moses at the burning bush is the same God who discovered us. Perhaps, it is in God's discovery of us that we begin to discover who we are in light of our destiny with God. God was at work in this young man's life, and I knew it not; just as I am so often unaware of what God is doing in my life.

The young man requested a visit from a chaplain (a minister), and that made all the difference in the world to him. I have not forgotten how his life touched mine.

Do you realize how healing your presence may be to another human being and how healing their presence may be for you?

Afterword

I hope that my second book, *Walking in Grandpa's Footsteps*, has in some way helped you to discover your stories of God's grace and mercy. Many stories are like nuggets of gold hidden in the sand: they wait to be discovered. Upon being discovered, go tell them on a mountaintop that all might hear of the great works that God has done in your life. I don't know of any better method of witnessing than telling your story.

If you have found some golden nuggets in this book, please tell family and friends. And I would greatly appreciate it, if you would take the time to write a book review and leave it on the website where you purchased this book. The more reviews, the greater the exposure of the book.

Thanks again to all of you who have taken the time to read this book. God willing, the next book will be entitled, *A Hobbit's View of God*. To write your comments and opinions of

Walking in Grandpa's Footsteps, go to the website where you purchased the book.

God's Blessings,

Robert Loran Ford

Reference List

A Feast of Families, by Virginia Stem Owens

A Hidden Wholeness, by Parker J. Palmer

A Serious Way of Wondering, by Reynolds Price

Christ & Culture, by H. Richard Niebuhr

Confessions of Saint Augustine, by Translated by Garry Wills

God of the Oppressed, by James H. Cone

Honest to God, by John A.T. Robinson

Know Your Story and Lead with It, by Richard L. Hester & Keli Walker-Jones

Man's Search for Meaning, by Viktor E. Frankl

Short Stories by Jesus, by Amy-Jill Levine

The Dead Sea Scriptures, English Translation by Theodor H. Gaster

The Masks We Wear, by Eugene C. Rollins

The Power of The Powerless, by Jürgen Moltmann

The Power to Bless, by Myron C. Madden

The Practice of the Presence of God, by Brother Lawrence

Whatever Became of Sin?, by Karl Menninger

Your God Is Too Small, by J.B. Phillips

What others are saying about,

Walking in Grandpa's Footsteps

"A child visits a sick friend! A Coke bottle breaks up a friendship! A family photo is taken! What could be intriguing, inspiring, or insightful about such common events? In Robert Ford's telling, these little stories hold profound truths. Tying story, song, and Scripture together, he has created another book that will make you want to turn the page quickly to read of the next event and its spiritual significance."

The Reverend Doctor Rick Jordan

Church Resources Coordinator

Cooperative Baptist Fellowship of North Carolina

"What is God's purpose for our lives? What gifts have we been given from God? How is our relationship with God? How are our relationships with family and others? Using humor and sincerity, Robert Loran Ford shares personal life experiences, and then encourages us to look more deeply into ourselves. He helps us see that God is always present and wants a personal relationship with each of us. By discovering who we are and can be through God's love for us, we may live a more fulfilling and content life. What a great book! It has made me laugh and it has pierced my heart."

Susan Steiger, M.S.Ed.

Hickory, North Carolina

About
Robert Loran Ford

Robert Loran Ford grew up on a cotton mill village in western North Carolina. He moved to Spartanburg, South Carolina, as a child, where Grace Baptist Church became a significant part of his life. He served in the United States Airforce and Army where he served as a chaplain. He is a graduate of Gardner Webb College and Southeastern Baptist Theological Seminary and has served as a pastor in both the Carolinas and as a Chaplain at Frye Regional Medical Center in Hickory, NC. He is also the author of *Behind Grandma's Apron Strings: Stories of Grace and Mercy* and coming soon, his third devotional book, *A Hobbit's View of God*.

Other Books by Robert Loran Ford

Ford, Robert Loran.

Hiding Behind Grandma's Apron Strings: Stories of Grace and Mercy

Coming Soon!

Ford, Robert Loran, *A Hobbit's View of God*

Don't miss out!

Visit the website below and you can sign up to receive emails whenever Robert Ford publishes a new book. There's no charge and no obligation.

https://books2read.com/r/B-A-DUUF-GGSR

BOOKS2READ

Connecting independent readers to independent writers.

www.ingramcontent.com/pod-product-compliance
Lightning Source LLC
Chambersburg PA
CBHW051650040426
42446CB00009B/1060